PRESERVING
MADE AT HOME

A FIREFLY BOOK

Published by Firefly Books Ltd. 2012

Copyright © 2012 Octopus Publishing Group Ltd.
Text copyright © 2012 Dick and James Strawbridge,
Jera Enterprises Ltd.

First printing

Publisher Cataloging-in-Publication Data (U.S.)

Strawbridge, Dick.
    Preserves : made at home / Dick and James
Strawbridge.
[176] p. : col. photos. ; cm.
Includes index.
Summary: An introduction to the art of preserving
foods, covering methods, equipment needed, and
recipes using the final products.
ISBN-13: 978-1-77085-079-8 (pbk.)
1. Canning and preserving. 2. Cooking (Canned foods).
3. Food – Preservation. I. Strawbridge, James. II. Title.
641.42 dc23   TX603.S763 2012

Library and Archives Canada Cataloguing in Publication

Strawbridge, Dick
    Preserving : made at home / Dick & James
Strawbridge.
Includes index.
ISBN 978-1-77085-079-8
    1. Canning and preserving. 2. Cooking (Canned
foods). 3. Food—Preservation. I. Strawbridge, James
II. Title.
TX603.S77 2012   641.4'2   C2012-900386-7

Published in the United States by
Firefly Books (U.S.) Inc.
P.O. Box 1338, Ellicott Station
Buffalo, New York 14205

Published in Canada by
Firefly Books Ltd.
66 Leek Crescent
Richmond Hill, Ontario L4B 1H1

Photography by Nick Pope

Printed and bound in China

Preserving was developed, designed and conceived by
Mitchell Beazley, an imprint of Octopus Publishing
Group Limited, Endeavour House, 189 Shaftesbury
Avenue, London, WC2H 8JY

Both metric and imperial measurements are given
for the recipes. Use one set of measures only, not a
mixture of both. Quantities for most dry ingredients
are listed by weight, since this provides greater
precision. However, approximate quantities by volume
are also listed.
Ovens should be preheated to the specified
temperature. If using a convection oven, follow the
manufacturer's instructions for adjusting the time and
temperature. Grills should also be preheated.

This book includes dishes made with nuts and nut
derivatives. It is advisable for those with known
allergic reactions to nuts and nut derivatives and
those who may be potentially vulnerable to these
allergies, such as pregnant and nursing mothers, the ill,
the elderly, babies and children, to avoid dishes made
with nuts and nut oils. It is also prudent to check
the labels of prepared ingredients for the possible
inclusion of nut derivatives.

The U.S. Food and Drug Administration and Health
Canada advise that eggs should not be consumed
raw. This book contains some dishes made with raw
or lightly cooked eggs. It is prudent for the more
vulnerable, such as pregnant and nursing mothers, the
sick, the elderly, babies and young children to avoid
dishes made with uncooked or lightly cooked eggs.

*Thank you to everyone who has
taken the time to teach us so that
we can now pass it on to Indy and
anyone else who will listen.*

PRESERVING
Made at Home

Dick & James
Strawbridge

FIREFLY BOOKS

CONTENTS

INTRODUCTION

There is nothing quite like a shelf or cupboard that is brimming with home-preserved products. Not all of us can grow or rear our own, but it is possible to make full use of seasonal food and store it for the rest of the year. It wasn't so long ago that every household had the skills to preserve and store its food -- indeed, it was a matter of life or death to ensure you had enough for your family to survive. We are fortunate enough to live in a time where our lives no longer revolve around providing food for the table, so we have passed responsibility to others for growing, rearing, finding, storing and even cooking our food. This convenience should not be undervalued, as it allows us time for leisure and the "good old days" were undoubtedly hard.

For many people, it is becoming increasingly important to know what they are eating and drinking: additives are treated with suspicion, so it's logical to want to make your own products. That being said, let's not forget the enjoyment that comes from putting delicious, homemade food on the table for friends and family. We are all used to mass-produced preserves that by their very nature have a consistent flavor, texture and appearance. Commercial producers have to ensure that their customers get what they expect every time, so all individuality is removed. With homemade preserves it is all but impossible to achieve exactly the same result every time. This variation is to be celebrated, and you may well find that the last jar of a favorite chutney made several years ago will be closely guarded and used in a positively miserly manner by your family. But don't worry, when it does finally disappear, another, probably very different, chutney will take over the mantle of being number one.

When you have a small selection of your own preserves at home, you will find it very easy to transform even the simplest meal or snack. A homemade cake filled with your own jam and a little cream or a simple lunch of bread, cheese or pâté and your own pickles or chutney will be savored because of all the effort that has been invested in the meal, albeit months in advance. If you're new to preserving, the tricky part is choosing where to begin and which methods to learn, and of course that will all depend on what your favorite preserves are. For us it's quite simple -- we have very eclectic tastes, so we'll try anything and everything.

SOURCING YOUR FOOD

It goes without saying that the better your fresh ingredients are, the better your preserves will be. The good news is that this doesn't mean you've got to track down special sources for exotic foods, or spend a fortune buying them. While it's true that supermarkets bring us every possible type of produce all year round, you will find that local seasonal food is undoubtedly superior. When you decide to preserve, it makes no sense to put all that effort into anything but the best quality you can lay your hands on, as it's very simply a matter of the final product reflecting what went in. True, flavors are enhanced and modified by the addition of sugar, salt, vinegars and spices, or they can be concentrated by drying. However, once you've opened that jar, it's no good wishing you'd done something different six months earlier.

There is also the matter of price: produce is cheapest when it is at its most abundant. It's a win/win situation -- you get the best choice and you pay less, so it would seem sensible to make the most of this great opportunity. If you grow your own -- and of course we recommend that you do -- you will have the happy problem of having to deal with gluts. There is always some point when the abundance of tomatoes, zucchini, apples, plums, gooseberries, strawberries or raspberries will mean you're not sure if you want to eat another, even though they are truly fantastic. These are the best moments to invest a little time in preserving the harvest for use at any time of year.

SKILLS AND FLAVORS

It is very important to remember that there are lots of possible variations when it comes to the methods and recipes in this book. Once you understand the principles, you can vary the flavors. You will have the joy of taking full credit for the magnificent preserves you produce, so feel free to fine-tune the recipes and make them your own.

In the following pages we show you how to make the most of seasonal produce when it is at its very best and most affordable. In return for a few hours' work, your homemade preserves will brighten up countless meals throughout the year, as well as making wonderful gifts. All you have to do is decide where you would like to begin, and you will soon find your pantry filling up with jarred, dried and bottled treats.

Dick & James

PREPARING TO

PRESERVE

Wondering where to begin? The great thing about preserves is the variety of products you can make, so the decision is all about what you really enjoy. Without a doubt, you should start by making something you love the taste of. If you have a sweet tooth, you could go for the old faithful of making strawberry jam, but you may do well to head a little out of your comfort zone and try a fruit cheese. They may not be as popular as jams, and the texture is slightly different, but a quince or damson cheese is a delight and the intensity of the fruit flavor is a wonderful thing. If you love your savories, a chutney or a pickle is a great route to achieving satisfaction -- however, you'll need to wait a while for the flavors to meld together and for your endeavors to reach their optimum.

STORAGE

Once you start making preserves, you will have the task of storing your creations – and it won't take long for you to amass shelves of jars. Space can be at a premium, and pantries tend to be only just big enough for storing the weekly shopping and the staples we take for granted. If you don't have much space in your kitchen, clean out an old cupboard or find a shelf in your garage. Anywhere that's clean, dry, sheltered and above the freezing point will do. Organization is important too, especially if you've stored your preserves in a more out of the way place. We label our jars carefully, date all of our preserves and arrange our shelves by product. You might believe you will remember exactly what you have made and where you've put it, but after six or nine months or even more, it is not surprising to forget. Keep a set of labels in one of your empty jars (you will find you'll begin to collect a supply) so they are always to hand when needed.

FRESH PRODUCE

It may seem unusual to have a section on storing fresh produce in a book on preserving. However, it is important to store food in a way that preserves the flavors and textures for as long as possible. Some vegetables store extremely well, and it is not necessary to process them prior to keeping them – it is more a matter of careful selection, a slight clean and then putting them in the right environment to prevent them from degrading.

It is all well and good telling you that most produce is best stored in a dark, dry and cool, but not freezing, location. In many homes, every effort is made to keep all areas light and warm, so you might need to find somewhere outside, unless you have a coldroom. The challenge of storing underground is to keep the area dry, but the upside is that the temperature stays pretty constant. Any place that is protected from the sun's heat and from frost in the winter – and, of course, drafts at any time of year – will make a great fresh produce store.

In most climates, outbuildings (or in our case an old outhouse) that have a good roof and are well insulated, along with windows that can be covered, make great stores. Sadly though, this rules out most backyard sheds, which tend to heat up with a little sunshine.

DRYING

Removing the moisture from produce is a preserving technique that has been used for millennia. The flavors are concentrated, and this is drying's strength. Anyone can preserve this way, and hanging herbs in your kitchen is a simple starting point. You can dry fruit, vegetables and spices outside, in a homemade solar dryer (see pages 38–41) or in an oven (convection ovens are particularly good), or you can use a food dehydrator.

JARS

Most of us have cupboards and fridges full of jars. If you're going to make your own jarred goodies, you will have to buy – or better yet, collect – a supply of jars to fill. There is a plethora of containers that can be bought specifically for preserving, lots of reusable jars with rubber seals, both clip-top and screw-lid, as well as artisan jam jars and no shortage of bargain jars, be they round, square or even hexagonal. Jars from our everyday shopping can be cleaned and reused. It's a little annoying if the lids are branded, but since many jar sizes are standardized, you will probably be able to find a plain lid that fits. Of course, saving jars in anticipation of filling them with preserves requires space. We have tried to keep ours in the garage or a shed but somehow they always get dusty and lids migrate away from the jars, so we now keep our supply in a cupboard in the kitchen or utility room.

As far as an essential kit goes, any large pan can be used for preserving, though there are special preserving pans available for those who intend to do a lot. Steer well clear of aluminium and invest in stainless steel – we picked up ours second hand. A preserving funnel is extremely useful as it has a wide neck to allow thick chutneys or jams to flow through and it stops a lot of mess and wastage. Buy one or make your own from the top of a plastic bottle.

BOTTLES

Learning to bottle your own syrups, sauces and alcoholic drinks is a natural progression from making your own jam or chutney. It's the cordials, syrups and

ketchups that are particularly satisfying to produce: you will have a collection of very handsome bottles that can be used at will, and they also make great presents. Yet again, it is extremely worthwhile to collect bottles for future use – especially elegant ones and those with ornamental stoppers.

The flavors of your homemade bottled treats will be unique and, of course, not exactly like those of commercially available products. This is particularly true when it comes to making your own cider, beer and wine, either from grapes or other fruit, flowers or herbs, but we consider the taste of our homemade alcoholic drinks to be well worth acquiring, and go through gallons of them.

Brewing and fermentation equipment is essential, so start collecting well in advance of when you intend to start. Masticators and presses can be shared or borrowed, so ask around and you could save yourself the cost. Stock up on bottle brushes and "magic balls" – little ball bearings that you swish around in the bottom of a glass container to scour away any dirt.

FREEZING

Not everything can be frozen, but freezing is a simple, effective and popular method of preserving food. Despite this, few people are actually good at it, as retaining the integrity and texture of meat, fruits or vegetables requires the correct techniques. Most households have a domestic freezer or at least a freezer compartment in their fridge, so you will require very little else to get started. The key is organization: if you don't use what you have put in the freezer while it is still at its best, you might as well not have bothered to freeze it. Label your freezer containers or bags effectively using a decent marker pen – write down the date as well as the contents – and make sure to visit your freezer regularly to use the goodies you have squirreled away. Any other items you need, such as pots and pans for blanching or trays on which to freeze produce, can be found in the average kitchen.

1

STORING FRESH PRODUCE

INTRODUCTION TO

STORING FRESH PRODUCE

Fruits and vegetables are always at their tastiest the moment they are picked. In fact, it's believed that it is best to harvest a leafy salad crop in the morning, when the sap is rising, and root vegetables in the evening, when the minerals are returning down into the main body of the plant. If you want to keep fresh produce in peak condition for as long as you can, it is very important to set up a good storage system. Here are a few essential rules to keep in mind.

GUIDELINES

- Take the time to trim off any leaves, stems and damaged bits before storing.
- Use a stiff brush to remove most of the soil clinging to root vegetables.
- Don't clean your produce with lots of water to remove all the mud, as it protects the skin; wipe clean with a dry cloth or papertowels instead.
- Discard anything that is damaged or diseased – it'll only get worse.
- Try to keep different fruits and vegetables spaced apart. The ethylene that develops from some produce can ripen others more quickly.
- Don't seal produce in plastic – unless you are keeping it in the fridge and using plastic bags specifically designed for food storage.
- Check stored produce regularly.
- Remove any produce that has gone moldy and think about what you can do to improve conditions.

LOCATION

The most important factor is accessibility. The last thing you want on a cold day is to have to go out in the rain and return to the kitchen wet and miserable, so store things inside or keep your storeroom close to the house.

TEMPERATURE

Temperature is extremely important in maintaining a successful storeroom. Most produce that you will store, with the exception of vegetables such as squashes and pumpkins, lasts longer in cool conditions. The ideal temperature range is between 0°C and 4.5°C (32°F and 40°F), so install a thermometer and check it regularly. During the warmer months you will want to draw cold air into your storeroom and keep that air inside, so it is worth installing an intake pipe low down in the room to draw in cold night air and another vent at its highest point to let out any warm air. This will help to encourage air circulation and improve ventilation (see page 21). Remember to screen these pipe openings to keep creatures at bay.

If you can set up your storeroom on a shady side of your house, you will be able to further

Nothing beats produce fresh from the garden

Every tomato has a use, some fresh, some preserved

STORING COMMON FRUITS AND VEGETABLES

PRODUCE	STORAGE METHOD	STORING TIME
Apples	Trays	3–4 months
Beets	Clamping	3–4 months
Carrots	Clamping	3–4 months
Garlic	Braiding	3–4 months
Jerusalem artichokes	Clamping	6 months+
Onions	Braiding	3–4 months
Pears	Trays	2–3 months
Potatoes	Clamping or sacks	3–6 months
Squashes	Trays	2–4 months

reduce the temperature. Another good idea is to install double doors to stop any warm summer air from getting in when you pay the storeroom a visit. Regular maintenance is vital if you want to run a really effective storeroom: watch the thermometer and open the cold air vents if it looks like the storeroom is getting too warm.

HUMIDITY

High humidity is best for the majority of stored produce. Aim for about 90–95%, as this will stop your food from shrivelling. If you'd like to work out the exact humidity of your storeroom, we recommend that you install a hygrometer, a specialist tool that measures humidity. Simply scattering water on the floor, or placing pans of water on the ground, is the easiest way to increase humidity levels. As a rule, earth floors are better for higher humidity levels than concrete. If your storeroom has an earth floor, cover it with gravel so that it is easy to spread water without getting your feet wet when you go to fetch something for dinner.

Another technique for keeping your vegetables looking fresh is to pack them in damp sawdust or sand. Avoid wrapping produce in plastic bags as this can quickly lead to stagnant air and surface mold growing on your harvest.

VENTILATION

Movement of air through and within your storeroom helps to remove any ethylene gas, which hastens the ripening process and can make produce smell bad or start sprouting. Leave gaps between your shelves and the wall so that air can circulate freely behind the produce. This will also reduce the risk of your fruits or vegetables developing mold.

If you are storing produce on a smaller scale in a cupboard, drill some holes in the door and cover them with fly screening – anything you can do to improve air-flow is good.

LIGHT

Almost all fruits and vegetables will store for longer if you keep them in the dark. The exceptions are onions and garlic, which may start to sprout, so it's better to keep them within easy reach in the kitchen.

SHELVING AND TRAYS

Make sure you incorporate plenty of useful storage space if you have a storeroom. We have found that slatted crates make great storage trays because they allow good air circulation and lots of them can be fitted tightly together. Avoid using metal shelving or treated wooden shelves (as there are chemicals in the preservatives), and instead use hard, durable woods such as oak, beech or chestnut. Try to make room for air to flow at the back of the shelves by leaving gaps. You can coat your shelves in plastic so that they are easy to wipe clean at the end of the season.

REFRIGERATION

Using a fridge to the best of its ability sounds like common sense, but it really is the 21st-century answer to storing most fresh garden produce. Keep the produce in your fridge in sealed plastic food storage bags, but use paper bags for mushrooms. Keep apples, avocados, melons and other ethylene-emitting produce away from ethylene-sensitive foods such as cucumbers, peppers, asparagus and members of the *Brassica* family, as it can result in yellowing, pitting and brown spots. Some foods also emit odors – a small bowl of baking soda kept in the fridge will help absorb any odors and moisture.

HANGING GARLIC

Garlic is easy to grow and very easy to cook with. We chop it into pesto, butter and dips, roast it in pans and even preserve it soaked in honey. Garlic can be used fresh and "wet," right out of the ground. But if you grow your own, you'll need a storage method that keeps it as fresh as possible. If you allow the outside to air-dry and hang garlic, either braided or bundled together, the cloves will retain their freshness for up to 6 months. The same method can be used to store onions and shallots.

PREPARING FRESH GARLIC

Indoors, garlic dries particularly well on simple trays with chicken-wire bases or wooden slats. We made several one year when we had a large garlic harvest, and stacked them on top of each other to save space. In good weather, you can allow the lifted garlic bulbs to lie on the ground outside to dry. However, sometimes it can be too wet and space may be at a premium, so you can move them to a corner of a polytunnel or greenhouse to speed up the process. You'll know the garlic is ready for the next stage when the stems are still flexible but yellow-brown and would easily light with a flame.

BRAIDING

It's easiest to braid sitting down. Select three bulbs and place them on your knees, with the stems pointing away from you. Braid the three together for a couple of centimeters (about an inch), keeping the bulbs close together and the weave tight. Add another bulb between two of the bulbs and repeat the braiding for another couple of centimeters. Keep going,

using your fingers to clamp the braid tight while you make a string with as many bulbs as you like. When you have finished, use a piece of string to tie the braided stems together and cut them to an appropriate length. Then tie a knot in the string and hang the garlic on a hook.

Anyone can braid

BUNDLING

A French-style "grappe" (meaning "bunch of grapes") is quicker and easier to make than a braid. All you do is join the bulbs together one at a time, keeping your finger and thumb clamped on the stems and tying each new bulb of garlic into the bundle with string. Stop when you get to about 6–10 bulbs and hang in the same way as a braid.

STORING

Hang your garlic in a light area with good air circulation. Keeping it on a hook by a kitchen window is ideal. Storing garlic in a dark place may accelerate the growing process and encourage it to sprout fresh green shoots. Consume within 6 months.

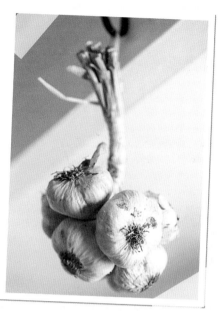

HOW TO MAKE A GRAPPE

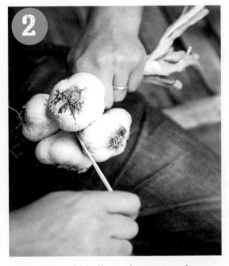

Tie a piece of string around the first bulb of garlic then use the string to make a figure-eight loop that weaves tightly around the neck of the next bulb, joining the two together.

Continue to add bulbs in this way until you have 6–10 bulbs of garlic in your grappe. Fasten off and make a loop that you can use to hang up the grappe.

METHOD #2

CLAMPING ROOT VEGETABLES

Clamping is a traditional storage technique that is very easy to do if you have a bit of space in your yard. It's a fantastic way to keep root vegetables, and we've been clamping produce since we started growing root crops, such as potatoes and parsnips, on a larger scale. Cover your pile of produce with sand, insulate with a layer of straw, then cover loosely with earth, allowing some air to reach the stored food -- your crops will keep for between 3 and 6 months.

PREPARING TO CLAMP

Clamped vegetables don't need to be completely clean, but they do need to be in perfect condition. You can give them a quick brush if you like, but the soil will help to preserve them for longer. Check each one carefully to make sure it is not damaged.

CLAMPING IN OPEN AIR

Harvest your vegetables, leave on top of the soil to dry for a couple of hours, then lay them on top of a layer of straw or bracken. Arrange them into a pyramid shape and cover with more straw. Leave them to sweat for 1 to 2 hours, then cover with 15 cm (6 inches) of earth. Allow some straw to poke through the soil and enable air to reach the crop. Pat the sides flat with a spade so they are steep and any rain can run off easily.

CLAMPING IN A BUCKET

Dig a hole in the ground and fill the base with a few stones. Drill several holes in the bottom of a bucket. Spread an 8 cm (3-inch) layer of sand or sawdust at the base of the bucket, followed by a single layer of vegetables. Cover with a layer of sand or sawdust and repeat the layers to fill the bucket. Place the bucket in the hole and cover with a 27 cm (11-inch) layer of straw and then a 5 cm (2-inch) layer of earth. This mulch will help to stop the vegetables from freezing over the winter (assuming the climate is not very cold). With smaller volumes of vegetables, you can store the bucket with its straw and earth mulch, uncovered, in a cellar or cool shed.

HOW TO CLAMP CARROTS

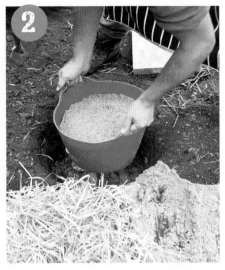

Put a layer of sand or sawdust in the bottom of your bucket and place a single layer of carrots on top of it.

Repeat these layers until you have filled the bucket, then put the bucket of carrots in a hole lined with some stones.

Cover the bucket with a thick layer of straw.

Now cover the straw with a layer of earth. Mark clearly where the carrots are being stored so that you don't forget.

STORING SQUASH & APPLES

Keeping produce fresh means that you have more time to use it and also an extended opportunity to decide how you want to preserve it. Squash are famously good for keeping in dry storage, as are apples. Apples that ripen early tend to be eaten right away, while later fruit is usually good to store. As with all stored and preserved produce, you will need to keep an eye on them.

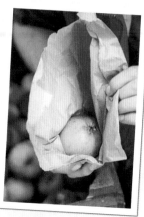

SETTING UP A STOREROOM

All you need to store fresh produce is a room with good air circulation and some shelves and trays. The amount of space you need will depend on how much you grow. To store, simply spread your produce out on a tray with a little separation between each item, and then place the tray on a shelf. Most shelving has enough of a gap between shelves for general household storage, but you might need to customize your shelving to meet your needs. Apples, for example, need only 10 cm (4 inches) between shelves, while the amount of room needed for squash will depend on the variety you grow.

Get into the habit of visiting your storeroom regularly. This will stop you from buying food you already have in stock and give you the opportunity to check that nothing is spoiling.

STORING SQUASH

A squash or pumpkin is ready to store when the skin is hard enough to withstand your

An easy way to check if a pumpkin is ready

fingernail being pressed into it, and when the stem connecting the fruit to the plant is shriveled up and dry. Be selective and avoid damaged ones. You can always make a soup with any squash that are not suitable for keeping and freeze it.

Place the perfect specimens on trays lined with newspaper or straw, and keep in a cool, dark place. Check regularly and discard any that show signs of collapse. If conditions are right, your harvest will keep well into the spring. (We rarely have any left by then, as they are too good to have sitting around.)

STORING APPLES

The old saying that it takes only one rotten apple to spoil the barrel is sadly true. Any apples that are visibly bruised or damaged

will go off and risk spoiling the rest of your crop. Therefore, select only the best-quality apples for keeping, and eat or cook with the rest.

Wrap the keepers individually in brown paper or newspaper. Try to use the palms of your hands instead of your fingertips to avoid damaging the fruit – you will be surprised how delicate some varieties are.

Place the wrapped apples either in apple trays or on shelves, making sure they do not touch each other to allow air to circulate and reduce the risk of spoiling.

SPICED APPLE SAUCE

This is a fantastic way to use your fresh apples. Delicious served on its own or with either roast pork or pheasant.

Makes 2.5 kg (5½ pounds)

25 g (1oz) butter (about 30 ml/2 tablespoons)

1 kg (2lb) apples, peeled, cored and chopped

1.25 kg (2¾ pounds) sugar (about 1,560 ml/ 6¼ cups)

500 ml (2 cups) apple cider

1 pinch each ground cinnamon, cloves and allspice

Melt the butter in a large pan, then add the apples and cook gently until softened. After a few minutes add the sugar and stir, then add the cider and spices. Bring to a boil, then reduce the heat to medium and simmer for 15 minutes. Strain through a sieve to remove excess liquid and store in a sterilized jar (see page 53) in the fridge.

2
DRYING

INTRODUCTION TO

DRYING

Drying is one of the oldest ways to preserve food. If done properly, using gentle heat, drying does not destroy as many of the nutrients as some of the other preserving techniques that require heat, such as canning and bottling. In warm climates, if food is harvested, laid out so that dry air can circulate around it and then left for a period of time, the air will take the moisture out. In cooler and more humid climates, however, it is important to monitor the conditions and, if necessary, assist the drying process.

HOW DRYING WORKS

The variety of foods that benefit from drying is impressive: you can dry cured meat, vegetables, herbs, spices, fruits and fungi. Taking the water out of produce deprives microorganisms (bacteria, yeast and mold) of the moisture they need in order to survive and spoil the food. It also prevents chemical reactions (enzymatic deterioration) from destroying the food during storage. Although drying itself does not destroy enzymes, most dried food is low enough in moisture to prevent enzymatic deterioration. If you can remove 80–90% of the moisture, the microbes are unable to perform.

Drying may prevent microbial growth, but bear in mind that there are chemical reactions caused by enzymes that can occur unless the food is pretreated before drying. Thankfully the enzymes in vegetables can be counteracted by simply blanching them (a quick immersion in boiling water or steam), and you can counteract the enzymes in fruit by treating the food with ascorbic acid, a form of vitamin C.

Dry at the lowest temperatures, otherwise the food will cook rather than dry. If the temperature is too high the cooking will cause the outside of the food to go hard and stop the moisture from escaping. Turning up the heat to reduce the drying time is therefore counterproductive. To speed up drying, low humidity is essential, and increasing the air-flow over the food surface is also beneficial.

DRYING METHODS

There are numerous ways of drying food: using the sun, leaving the food out in the fresh air for a period of time, or using a commercial dehydrator. We have hung things up to dry in porches, used our convection oven with and without heat and have built solar dryers (see pages 38–9), though they are only really effective in hot weather Generally, air drying is complete in 2 or 3 days, depending on conditions (see pages 34–5).

FRUIT DRYING

Ripe fruits are best, but try not to use any that are too ripe or overripe, as the results will not be as high in quality. There are no hard and fast rules about how to slice fruit for drying. Some fruits (such as figs and berries) are best dried whole, but generally thin, even, peeled pieces dry the fastest. You can leave the peel

Colorful and healthy — dried root vegetables
are full of flavor and goodness

DRYING COMMON FRUITS AND VEGETABLES

FOOD	PREPARATION	TREATMENT	DRYING TIME
Apples	Peel, core and cut into rings or slices	Dip in lemon or orange juice for 4 minutes	4–6 days
Figs	None	None	4–5 days
Grapes	Choose seedless varieties	Blanch for 30 seconds	3–5 days
Eggplants	Cut into 5 mm (¼-inch) slices	Blanch for 4 minutes	6–8 days
Green beans	Wash and cut into short lengths	Blanch for 2 minutes	8–10 days
Mushrooms	Brush any compost off the mushrooms and slice large ones	None	6–8 days
Onions	Slice about 3 mm (⅛ inch) thick	None	8–11 days
Peppers	Cut into 3 mm (⅛ inch) rings	None	6–8 days
Parsley	Wash and cut along stalks lengthways	None	6–8 days

on, but the process will take a little longer. Prior to drying, some sliced fruits should be dipped in orange or lemon juice for a few minutes (see table above). As there are sugars in fruit, it can become sticky as it dries, so use a nonstick baking sheet or cover your baking sheet with parchment paper. Place items in a single layer and avoid overlapping.

VEGETABLE DRYING
Onions, peppers, celery and mushrooms are all well suited to drying. First cut the vegetables into pieces of uniform size and thickness. If they need to be blanched (see table above), immerse the vegetables in boiling water for a couple of minutes, then strain through a sieve and immediately immerse in iced water to stop the cooking process. Drain, then dry.

HERB DRYING
The best time to harvest most herbs for drying is just before the flowers open, when the buds are about to burst. Drying can take 2 or 3 weeks, depending on the conditions. Rinse the herbs in cold water, and then shake

off any excess. Those with long stems can be dried in bunches. Tie the stems together and hang them upside down where there is plenty of room for air to circulate. If where you intend to hang them in is dusty, you can place each bunch in a paper bag with some holes cut in it – the air should still circulate, but the dust will not settle on the herbs. Large-leaved herbs, such as basil, or those with short stems can be dried on a rack or tray. If you use a rack, turn the herbs over daily.

FOOD DEHYDRATORS

Food dehydrators are small electrical appliances for drying foods indoors and have a heater and a fan. They are efficient and reliable, but make sure you get one that is big enough for your needs. Remember that your oven can also be used as a food dehydrator. Convection ovens are even better.

DRYNESS TESTING

Make sure your food is thoroughly dried before storing. The best way to determine the dryness of the food is to consider its look, feel and taste. Take several pieces of food and cut through the center of the thickest part. There should be no visible signs of moisture (a dark center means the food needs to dry for longer). Check the following:

- Fruits should be pliable and springy, and should not stick together if folded over on themselves.
- Vegetables should be brittle, as if they would shatter if hit with a hammer.
- Meats should feel very dry, and jerky, for example, should be dark, fibrous and form sharp points when bent.
- Herbs should be brittle and should crumble if rubbed in the palms of the hands.
- Fruit leathers should be dry to the touch and peel away easily from the tray.

STORING

Having achieved the dryness you are after, it's important to store what you have made. Sterilized sealable jars are the perfect way to store your dried produce (see page 53).

AIR DRYING

Air drying is one of the simplest and most decorative methods of preserving. Not all fruits and vegetables are suited to it, but there are some that will transform your kitchen into a hanging garden of edible decorations. Every year we especially like to hang up chilies and herbs ready for use during the winter. By removing moisture there is far less chance of your produce spoiling before you get the chance to use it, and the drying process can also intensify the flavor, which will be released when the dried ingredient is added to your cooking.

DRYING CHILIES

Use string to tie the chilies into clusters of three or four at regular intervals then suspend the clusters in a line, using hooks. Alternatively, pass a needle and thread through the stems. This way you'll end up with a long, even line of chilies with plenty of room for air to circulate.

Start by choosing a good place to hang your chilies. An airing cupboard could dry them in a few days, and somewhere in the kitchen (ideally not in a corner as that can hinder air circulation) can air-dry herbs or chilies in 2–3 weeks. If you have a porch or shed, try hanging a string of chilies under the eaves. The key is for the chilies to remain dry but have good air circulation around them. We've learned from experience that although drying above the oven looks great, and they can dry more quickly thanks to the extra heat, it's not worth doing because the chilies get covered in an oily residue from the pans cooking below.

Leave for 2–3 weeks, or until they are dry. Check them every couple of days. When the chilies are so dry that the pods snap instead of bend, they can be stored in glass jars. Keep in a dark, cool place.

Any knot will do the job ⟋

LAZY CHILI FLAKES

150 ml (⅔ cup) vinegar

30 ml (2 tablespoons) sugar

50 g (2 ounces) dried chilies, stems removed

1 pinch salt

1 pinch freshly ground black pepper

Put the vinegar and sugar into a pan and heat gently until the sugar has dissolved. Blitz the chilies in a food processor, or grind them using a pestle and mortar, until flaky, and add to the vinegar. Bring to a boil, then allow to cool in the pan. Season with salt and pepper, then pour into a jam jar, seal tightly and store in the fridge.

There's a lot of heat in this jar

DRYING HERBS

For the most intense flavor, pick herbs such as sage, rosemary and thyme just before they flower, wrap their stems tightly with string and hang them in small bunches somewhere airy. Once dry, take them down and pluck the leaves from the stems. Put the aromatic leaves into jars and keep close to the stove for ready-to-use flavor impact.

If you don't grow your own herbs, ask neighbors or friends whether you could harvest some herbs from their garden, as most herbs will benefit from the occasional trim. You could buy bunches of herbs for drying, but that's not an economical option.

Dried chilies are integral to much of the cooking that we enjoy. This recipe combines dried chili flakes with herbs and makes a very tasty barbecue kebab. Using the entire chili, seeds and all, gives this dish plenty of heat.

Serves 4-8

400 g (14 ounces) monkfish tail, cubed
400 g (14 ounces) salmon fillet, cubed
100 g (3½ ounces) large tiger shrimp
juice of 1 lime

For the chili and herb rub

4 dried chilies, finely chopped
2 garlic cloves, finely chopped
15 ml (1 tablespoon) chopped fresh lemon thyme
15 ml (1 tablespoon) chopped fresh parsley

zest of 1 lime
5 ml (1 teaspoon) sea salt
5 ml (1 teaspoon) freshly ground black pepper
30 ml (2 tablespoons) olive oil

For the sweet chili sauce

2 dried red chilies, finely chopped
1 garlic clove, crushed
30 ml (2 tablespoons) sugar
60 ml (¼ cup) water
20 ml (4 teaspoons) white wine vinegar
5 ml (1 teaspoon) cornstarch

SEAFOOD KEBABS WITH CHILI & HERB RUB

Put eight wooden skewers to soak in cold water for at least 30 minutes.

To make the chili and herb rub, place the chilies, garlic, thyme and parsley in a large bowl with the lime zest, salt and pepper. Add the olive oil and stir well.

Add the fish and shrimp to the bowl, stirring thoroughly to make sure everything is completely coated with the spicy rub. Heat your barbecue or grill, and while it is heating up, thread the chili fish and shrimp onto skewers.

To make the sweet chili sauce, put the chilies and garlic into a small pan. Add the sugar, vinegar and water and bring to a boil. Reduce the heat and simmer for 3–4 minutes. Finally, mix the cornstarch to a paste with 15 ml (1 tablespoon) of water and stir into the sauce until incorporated.

Cook the kebabs over or under high heat for 5 minutes – watch them carefully to avoid burning. Serve with the sweet chili sauce and a squeeze of fresh lime juice.

Thread Kebabs carefully

METHOD #5

SOLAR DRYING

Solar drying is a preserving method that's been around for thousands of years, and it has begun to make a comeback. At its simplest, solar drying can be done with virtually no equipment -- all you need is air-flow around your chosen fruit or vegetable, and then it's a matter of letting nature take its course. We built our own solar dryer to improve our ability to store ripe garden produce, such as tomatoes, chilies and apples, and to save money on luxury sun-dried foods. We're big fans of this method of drying produce -- no fuel is required, so the dryer costs nothing to run.

ADVANTAGES AND DISADVANTAGES

- Solar dryers are really easy to build in a couple of hours from cheap materials.
- They are great for summer preserving as they don't contribute unwanted heat inside the house.
- Solar drying is completely free, using no fuel other than the power of the sun.
- Solar dryers take longer than a conventional oven to dry food, so preparation has to be done several hours – or even days – before you intend to eat your produce. But there is no real supervisory cooking time, so we enjoy the time off.
- Cloudy and rainy weather seriously impairs performance, so solar dryers are only a sunny weather option.

HOW A SOLAR DRYER WORKS

A solar dryer consists of a solar collector, a glass-covered box lined with black, heat-absorbing material (usually a piece of metal, as it's particularly effective at absorbing heat). The solar dryer is angled towards another box – the solar oven – which contains a metal rack, and the heat collected filters upwards to dry the food placed on the rack. The inside walls of the solar oven are painted white so that heat loss is minimized and the warmth is retained in the drying area. The performance of a solar dryer is much slower than that of a conventional gas or electric oven, but as an inexpensive way to preserve produce it is unbeatable.

MAKING A SOLAR DRYER

The first stage is to construct your solar collector, which is essentially a large wooden box with a glass front. The wood helps to insulate the box and keep in the heat. To save time, use an old glass-fronted cupboard to build your solar dryer, or reuse an old wooden box or drawer with an old window fitted over it. The bigger the better for this part of the solar dryer, as you will be able to collect more sunshine and therefore dry food more quickly as a result. Remove one end of the box. Then drill holes in the other end and

Metal drying rack

Batten support for rack

Warmed air rises through the dryer

Holes covered with fine screening

Cold air enters the dryer

Swivel cover for air flow

Corrugated iron painted black

Interior painted white

Glass

Wooden spacer to increase air flow

cover them with fine screen to prevent insects from getting into the system. These holes allow air to be drawn in at the base, and this is warmed inside the collector before rising into the oven through the open end that will eventually sit on top. Close up any other holes and gaps. Paint the inside of the box white, and tack on a small blocks of wood to act as spacers for air to circulate around the black material to be fitted next.

Cut a piece of metal, preferably corrugated iron, to fit into the box and paint it black. Place this piece of black material inside the box, sitting it on the spacers. Cover the box with a hinged glass panel or old window. Position the solar collector so that it is directly facing the midday sun and build a support for it to keep it at the correct height and angle. This structure will also support the oven or drying box.

The next step is to build a very simple box to fit above the solar collector. This will be the oven where you put food to dry. Paint the inside of your oven white so that heat doesn't radiate outside when it heats up. Position battens on either side of the oven for placing wire trays or grills on. Drill several holes in the lower front edge of the oven so that they line up with the open end of your solar collector. Seal the two sections together with screws, making sure that there aren't any gaps. Drill a vent hole at the top of the box. Then make a swivel cover by attaching a small doorknob to a piece of wood big enough to cover the vent and screwing one corner to the box.

WHERE TO POSITION IT

Food in a solar dryer doesn't reach very high temperatures, so if you want to dry something and eat it the same day, it's best to start drying before noon and continue all day. Place your solar dryer in direct sunlight facing south. You'll need to move it every couple of hours to track the direction of the sun and avoid shadows from surrounding objects, but if you don't have time for this, simply position it facing where the sun will be at its highest point. Drying times depend hugely on the specific shape, size and design of your solar dryer, and, of course, on the weather. The hours before and after midday tend to be the most effective for drying food.

USING THE SOLAR DRYER

We recommend using a solar dryer for drying fruit, vegetables, seeds and herbs. Complex dishes can be cooked in a solar dryer, but you really need a very hot, sunny day to achieve good results.

Before drying, remember to make sure you cut the food into smaller pieces than normal, as a larger surface area yields better results. If the cut fruit or vegetable would normally discolor when left in the air, it will also do that in the solar dryer. To prevent this, rub the sliced food with lemon juice or ascorbic acid before you put it in the dryer.

Don't be tempted to turn the food or peek

HOW TO USE A SOLAR DRYER

Spread out a layer of the food on your grill and place it in the dryer – make sure the grill sits well off the oven floor as the air needs to circulate all around the food.

Put the lid on the dryer and leave until the food has dried.

at what is cooking inside your dryer as this will allow precious heat to escape and slow down the whole process. The usual temperature achieved by our solar dryer are around 50°C (120°F), which is ideal for drying herbs.

OTHER DESIGNS

There are many different designs of solar dryer. Another of our favorites is based on the idea of reflecting the sun's rays on to a focused spot in order to achieve higher temperatures. Take an old satellite dish and cover it in aluminum foil. Face it towards the sun and hang a kettle above it to boil water for a cup of tea!

SUN-DRIED TOMATOES

Thinly slice your tomatoes. Lay these on a wire tray, put them in the solar dryer and dry them in the midday sun for 4-5 hours. When ready to eat, they should feel completely dry and chewy. If they haven't reached that point, remove them from the solar dryer, place them in an airtight container overnight, and repeat the drying process the next day. Depending on the sun, it could take a couple of days or even up to a week to dry the tomatoes. When finished, place them in a jar with olive oil or seal in an airtight container, and place in a dark cupboard. They can be stored for up to 6 months. Rehydrate in warm water for 1 hour before using, or use straight from the oil.

SUN-BLUSHED TOMATOES

Sun-blushed tomatoes are simply partially dried. Follow the instructions for sun-dried tomatoes but remove them from the dryer after the first 4-5-hour drying session. Store them in the fridge with a drizzle of oil and consume within a week.

sun-blushed tomatoes with a little salt

We love this granola -- it's like a breakfast cereal that has been crossed with a pancake. The fruit and nut combinations are completely yours to decide on -- try hazelnuts, Brazil nuts, pumpkin seeds or sunflower seeds. The ratio of roughly equal parts cereal to fruit and nuts keeps a good balance, but otherwise it is all down to personal choice and whatever you've stored in your pantry.

Makes about 1.35 kg (3 pounds)

150 ml (⅔ cup) canola oil

100 ml (scant ½ cup) hot water

200 ml (⅞ cup) honey

500 g (1 pound) rolled oats

300 g (10 ounces) nuts (sliced almonds, chopped pecans and chopped walnuts)

200 g (7 ounces) dried fruit (raisins, golden raisins and dried cherries)

LUXURY GRANOLA

Preheat the oven to 160°C (325°F).

Place the oil, hot water and honey in a bowl and whisk to combine. Put the oats and nuts in a large bowl and mix together. Pour in the honey mixture and stir until the oats and nuts are evenly coated.

Spread the mixture on to two baking sheets. Bake in the oven for 10 minutes, then remove, stir, put back into the oven and bake for another 10 minutes or until toasted.

The mixture will harden as it cools. Once the granola has cooled completely, break apart any large lumps, stir in the dried fruit and store in an airtight container at room temperature for up to 2 months. Alternatively, you can freeze the granola for up to 6 months.

OVEN DRYING

Oven drying food is a really effective way to preserve produce beyond its natural growing season and effectively prevents the development of unwanted enzymes, bacteria, yeasts and fungi that thrive on moisture. Not only does dried produce last longer, it often has a more intense flavor, and you can eat sweet summer fruits and autumnal treats in the heart of winter. On the financial front, drying your own fruits and vegetables is a fantastic way to enjoy luxury ingredients, such as dried mushrooms, chilies and sun-dried tomatoes, at a fraction of the cost – especially if you use the residual heat in the oven after cooking a meal or baking a cake.

CHOOSING YOUR PRODUCE

We only ever dry the freshest, healthiest and most prolific of our fruits and vegetables, and make sure we use sharp tools when harvesting to avoid bruising the produce. Try to time it so that you harvest when the plants are not covered in dew and moisture, as this will slow down the drying time – wait until the afternoon for best results.

DRYING

To dry fruit and vegetables, you have to slice them, spread them on trays and heat them at a low temperature for a long time. Removing the moisture slowly in a conventional electric oven for a few hours at about 45–55°C (113–130°F) works well. If your oven doesn't go down to 50°C, set it to its lowest temperature and leave the door open. Dry several things at once to make full use of the heat.

IS IT READY YET?

Testing to see when your produce is dried is a simple matter of trial and error. Dry your food for a few hours and then test to see if it needs longer. If it does, leave it in the oven for another hour and test again. Repeat until the food is dry. Try to close the door quickly after checking in order to save the stored heat.

With plants such as herbs or chilies, test them by bending them in your hand – if they snap, they're ready, if they bend, leave them for a little longer. With some produce, including most fruits, you will know it is ready if you squeeze it and no juice comes out.

STORING

Storage containers are a key part of the drying process. Airtight containers, food-grade plastic bags and glass jars are all good ways to store your dried foods. We save almost every glass jar that comes into the house, cleaning and reusing them for storing our dried produce. If you are planning to dry in bulk, large rubber-sealed jars are a good investment.

NOW TRY: APPLE & PEAR RINGS

Core the fruit, cut it into 5 mm (¼-inch) thick rings, and then dip them into a solution of water, lemon juice, a spoonful of sugar and a pinch of ground cinnamon. Blot off any excess liquid with papertowels and place your rings on a rack in the oven at about 45–55°C (113–130°F) for 3–5 hours. When they are ready they can be eaten dry as a snack or used in recipes. Store for 3–6 months.

NOW TRY: ROOT CHIPS

Beets, parsnips and carrots all make excellent chips, and luckily this healthy snack is easy to make. Clean the vegetables, then slice thinly, place on a baking sheet and put them in the oven at about 45–55°C (113–130°F) for 3–5 hours. When they are ready, place in an airtight container and store for 3–6 months.

NOW TRY: HERBS & SPICES

Dry leafy herbs, such as rosemary and sage, just before they flower. This is when their oils are at the highest level and the leaves are highly aromatic. Arrange your herbs on a baking sheet and dry in the oven at 40°C (105°F) for 2–3 hours. Once dried, hold them over a piece of paper and crumble between your fingers to remove the leaves from the stems. Tip the herbs into an airtight container and store in a dark place for up to 6 months. The same process can be used for drying the seeds of herbs such as coriander and cumin. A maximum temperature of 47°C (115°F) is the ideal, as the aromatic oils can be damaged by higher temperatures.

Crumble and store

In most climates, home-grown strawberries are abundant in the summer months but unavailable for the rest of the year, so we like to make them into a snack that will last a little longer than the fresh fruit. The secret is slow cooking at a very low temperature. This recipe works well with any soft fruit, so you can experiment with other ingredients too.

Serves 4

300 g (10 ounces) strawberries

50 g (2 ounces) sugar (about 60 ml/ ¼ cup)

STRAWBERRY LEATHER FRUIT SNACK

Preheat your oven to 50°C (122°F) or its lowest temperature.

Now put the strawberries in a bowl and crush or blend them until they're fairly smooth but with a bit of texture remaining. Add the sugar to the bowl and stir well.

Spread the fruit mixture on to a piece of parchment paper or a nonstick baking sheet and place in the oven for 6–8 hours.

Let cool on the parchment paper or baking sheet, then cut into long, thin strips and peel each strip off individually. Roll each strip up and store in an airtight container for up to 3 months.

3

JARS

INTRODUCTION TO

JARS

A glass jar with a sealed lid is the perfect container in which to keep food for long periods of time. There is something very satisfying about going to the pantry and choosing from a plethora of colorful jars, all of which you have lovingly filled. When you take control of your pantry and know exactly what has gone into each recipe, you can rustle up a meal that represents the very best of home cooking. There are a number of ways to prepare food to be stored in jars; in this section we cover preserving in brine, vinegar, oil, sugar and alcohol. Some produce lends itself to a specific type of treatment, but each method produces its own distinct flavors and textures.

KEY METHODS

The method we focus on here involves storing home-processed food in sterilized glass jars. Food that should be preserved in this way has high acidity (a pH of more than 4.6), and high salt or sugar content, for example jams, pickles and chutneys, as well as most fruits.

For the record, there is also a method whereby home-processed food is preserved by sealing it in mason jars. This is called "canning," and the food can have a shelf-life of 1–5 years. Food that should be preserved in this way has low acidity (a pH of less than 4.6) and includes most vegetables as well as meat and poultry. If not done correctly, home canning can expose you to botulism (a serious form of food poisoning), so the food must be brought to a high enough temperature (116–130°C/240–265°F) for long enough to kill the microorganisms that carry disease. As you don't want to the food to become unpalatable and lose all nutritional value, you should aim to get a temperature of 121°C (250°F) for 3 minutes, using a large, robust pressure cooker designed for the job.

CHOOSING YOUR JARS

Numerous specialty stores tempt us with gorgeous jars filled with artisan-made jams, chutneys, pickles, mustards ands sauces. If you agree that there is something rather decadent about paying exorbitant amounts for such prettily packaged products, you will immediately understand how your own jars filled with delicious products can make excellent presents – the perfect combination of luxury and thoughtfulness. Always keep your eyes out for attractive jars that will make unique gifts.

Before you launch yourself into filling every available jar you can find, it's important to understand why certain things are essential. First, the food must be treated or processed so that the microorganisms that can cause it to spoil are unable to function. Second, the jars must be sterilized to ensure that the jams, pickles and preserves you spend a lot of time making will keep well. Jars that have not been sterilized properly will infect the food inside so that it will spoil very quickly and have to be thrown away.

Herb-infused oils look good and taste great

Every bit of juice goes into a marmalade

HOW TO STERILIZE JARS

There are numerous ways of sterilizing jars, but we find the following method to be extremely effective.

- Heat the oven to 140°C (275°F).
- Arrange the jars and lids on the oven shelf, making sure they are not touching each other.
- Always prepare more jars (and lids) than you think you will need. Should you end up with more mixture than anticipated, it is too late to start sterilizing more jars once the food is ready.
- Check the lids to ensure they are free from nicks and cracks, otherwise they may not be airtight.
- Close the oven door and leave the jars to heat up for about 20 minutes.
- If using a funnel to fill your jars, be sure to sterilize it too (if the funnel is made of plastic, sterilize it by immersing it in boiling water for a few minutes).

HOW TO FILL JARS

- Using thick oven mitts, remove each jar from the oven as needed and put it on to a heatproof mat or a large pot holder.
- Make sure you fill the jar while the preserve is as hot as the glass.
- Do not add cold food to hot jars, or hot food to cold jars, otherwise the jars might crack.
- Leave a little "headspace" at the top of each jar before you seal it – it's necessary to ensure a secure vacuum seal.

HOW TO SEAL JARS

- Always wipe the rim of the jar before you seal it, because any food debris or traces of salt left behind will prevent the lid from sealing properly.

- Leave jams, preserves or pickles to settle for 15 minutes with the lids just sitting on the top before sealing.
- Make sure to label and date your jars – it will make managing your store cupboard much easier in the long run.

HOW TO CHECK JAR SEALS

When hot food is put into a sterilized jar and the lid is screwed down (or, if you are using clip-top jars similar to the ones illustrated below, when the hinged lid is snapped into place over the sealing ring), the air in the gap above the content will contract as it cools, creating an airtight seal. Lots of modern jar lids have dimples that are pulled down when this happens, and if you press on the lid, there should be no popping noise. If it does move and "pop," the contents may not be safe to eat. The lid of a securely sealed jar will always be firmly sucked down onto the top of the jar.

METHOD #7

PICKLING

Cold pickling preserves the texture and appearance of your ingredients, so cold-pickled cucumbers, for example, retain their vibrant color and crispness. The preparation involved in making cold pickles is largely to do with getting the vegetables ready -- peeling, chopping and slicing them as necessary. The basic technique requires the use of salt to draw out as much moisture as possible from the vegetables before you pump them full of the preserving power of vinegar and the flavor of pickling spices.

HOW TO MAKE PICKLES

Slice your cucumbers into thin strips and layer them in a bowl or plastic container. Cover lightly with salt, put some garlic cloves on top, followed by more salt. Repeat the layers and leave overnight.

Rinse thoroughly, then place in sterilized jars (see page 53). Mix the shallots, vinegar, bay leaf, herbs and mustard seeds in a jug, then pour over the cucumbers, making sure to fill the jar. Seal the jar, leave the pickles to infuse with flavor and enjoy 3–4 weeks later.

PREPARING FLAVORINGS

If you want to save time when pickling, it is worth making a batch of pickling spices and storing them in their own clearly labelled jar. A classic pickling spice recipe would include a variety of broken and crumbled herbs and spices, the more fragrant the better. Some of our favorite flavorings are mustard seeds, black peppercorns, whole cloves, allspice, mace, bay, ginger, coriander seeds and cinnamon sticks.

MAKING YOUR PICKLES

Start by preparing your vegetables. Cut off any stalks or roots then carefully peel, chop and slice the vegetables as required. Start layering them in a bowl or plastic container with thin layers of salt in between. Repeat this process until all the vegetables that you want to pickle are covered in salt. Leave overnight at room temperature.

The next morning, wash off the excess salt under running water. Pack the vegetables into sterilized jars (see page 53), mix your vinegar and flavorings together, then pour the mixture over the vegetables in the jars, making sure they are fully submerged.

Seal the jars and store for at least a few weeks before enjoying. Cold pickles will keep for 6 months.

PICKLES

Makes 500 g (1 pound)

500 g (1 pound) knobbly cucumbers, finely sliced into long, thin strips

200 g (7 ounces) salt (about 250 ml/1 cup)

2 garlic bulbs, cloves peeled

3 shallots, finely sliced

800 ml (3¼cups) white wine vinegar

1 bay leaf, crumbled

30 ml (2 tablespoons) chopped fresh dill or tarragon

10 ml (2 teaspoons) mustard seeds

Follow the instructions opposite to make pickles.

PICKLED ONIONS

Makes 1 kg (2 pounds)

1 kg (2 pounds) onions, peeled

100 g (3½ounces) salt (about 125 ml/½cup)

200 g (7 ounces) sugar (about 250 ml/1 cup)

1 L (4 cups) malt vinegar

5 ml (1 teaspoon) coriander seeds

5 ml (1 teaspoon) yellow mustard seeds

5 ml (1 teaspoon) whole allspice

5 ml (1 teaspoon) black peppercorns

2 dried chilies

Sprinkle the onions with salt and leave overnight. Rinse and put them into sterilized jars (see page 53). Place the sugar and vinegar in a pan and heat until the sugar has dissolved. Add the pickling spices, then pour over the onions. For best results, leave for 1 month before eating.

METHOD #8

HOT PICKLING

As the name suggests, hot pickling involves applying heat to at least some of the ingredients. A good example of this technique is pickled limes, which, like many pickles made from fruit, is intended to alleviate the heat of curries. There are any number of variations, but it's all up to personal taste. The texture is determined by the size of the pieces of citrus fruit. Thin slices or smaller chunks will soften more during the cooking process (a lime cut into 16 pieces will be thinner and softer than one cut into 8). Not surprisingly, the hotness of the pickle can be changed by simply varying the amount of chili used (75 ml/⅓ cup makes it nice and tangy, but 150 ml (⅔ cup) or more and the pickle becomes seriously hot).

Hot and tangy

HOT PICKLED LEMONS

Lemons can be used instead of limes, but they break down more quickly so the texture is softer.

1 kg (2 pounds) lemons

100 g (3½ ounces) salt

45 ml (3 tablespoons) mustard seeds

10 fenugreek seeds

10 ml (2 teaspoons) cumin seeds

5 ml (1 teaspoon) cardamom seeds

400 g (14 ounces) sugar (about 500 ml/2 cups)

75 ml (⅓ cup) chili powder

3 garlic cloves

2 ml (½ teaspoon) asafetida

The method is the same as for pickled limes (just follow the instructions opposite).

HOT PICKLED LIMES

1 kg (2 pounds) limes (about 16)

100 g (3½ ounces) salt
(about 125 ml/½ cup)

45 ml (3 tablespoons) mustard seeds

10 fenugreek seeds

10 ml (2 teaspoons) cumin seeds

5 ml (1 teaspoon) cardamom seeds

400 g (14 ounces) sugar
(about 500 ml/2 cups)

75 ml (⅓ cup) chili powder

75 g (3 ounces) fresh ginger, grated

To make the lime pickle, follow the instructions opposite.

HOW TO MAKE HOT PICKLED LIMES

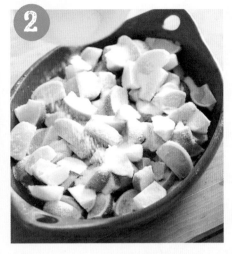

Soak the limes overnight in a bowl of cold water. Drain the limes, then cut the top and bottom off of each. Chop the fruit into pieces, removing the pits to avoid bitterness.

Place the limes in a large bowl and sprinkle with the salt. Leave for several hours so that the moisture is drawn out of the limes.

Mix the aromatic seeds together. Pour the liquid from the bowl of limes into a pan, and add the seeds and sugar. Slowly bring to a boil, stirring until the sugar dissolves.

Boil for 1 minute then remove from the heat and add the chili. When cool, stir in the lime wedges and ginger. Pour into sterilized jars (see page 53). Keep in a warm place for 4 or 5 days, and then store in a cool, dark place for 4 weeks.

The velvety sauce and crisp vegetables are what make a good piccalilli so special, and this recipe has both. We love it with cheese, cold meats and sausages -- the list is endless.

Makes 2.5-3 kg (5½-6½ pounds)

1 cauliflower, broken into small florets

1 zucchini, cut into 1 cm (½-inch) dice

3 medium onions, cut into 1 cm (½-inch) dice

3 carrots, cut into 1 cm (½-inch) dice

1 cucumber, peeled, seeded and cut into 1 cm (½-inch) dice

200 g (7 ounces) green beans, cut into 1 cm (½-inch) pieces

100 g (3½ ounces) salt (about 125 ml/½ cup)

75g (2½ ounces) flour (about 150 ml/⅔ cup)

15 ml (1 tablespoon) mild curry powder

15g (½ ounce) ground turmeric (about 30 ml/ 2 tablespoons)

45g (1¾ ounces) mustard powder (about 110 ml/ scant ½ cup)

25g (1 ounce) ground ginger (about 75 ml/⅓ cup)

1 L (4 cups) white (distilled) malt vinegar

600g (1¾ pounds) sugar (about 750 ml/3 cups)

PICCALILLI

Put all the prepared vegetables in a large bowl, toss with the salt, then cover and leave for 24 hours. Rinse well in several changes of water and leave them to drain in a colander for 30 minutes.

Sift the flour and spices into a large pan and gradually start to add the vinegar, blending well until you have a smooth paste with no lumps. Add the rest of the vinegar and the sugar and bring to a boil, stirring all the time, until thick. Add the prepared vegetables and bring back to a boil for 2 minutes.

Remove the pan from the heat, pour the piccalilli into sterilized jars (see page 53) and seal. Leave for at least 1 month to mature before eating.

The jars should keep, unopened, for 18 months if stored in a cool dark place. Once opened, keep in the fridge for up to 6 weeks.

Fresh and crispy vegetables

Sometimes we all need a satisfying bite in a hurry. This recipe for sauerkraut is much quicker than the traditional fermentation method. We make a batch of it every so often to eat in a sausage sandwich, or to serve with roast pork.

Serves 4

15 ml (1 tablespoon) olive oil

1 onion, thinly sliced

1 white cabbage, shredded

300 ml (1¼ cups) apple apple cider vinegar

125 ml (½ a cup) cider

15 ml (1 tablespoon) salt

QUICK SAUERKRAUT

Heat the oil in a heavy-bottomed pan then add the onion and cook until it softens. Add the cabbage, vinegar, cider and salt and bring to a boil. Simmer for about 30 minutes, adding water if it gets too dry.

Stored in a sterilized jar (see page 53), this simple sauerkraut will keep for 2 weeks in the fridge.

Pour in the apple cider vinegar

FLAVORED VINEGARS

Any bottle will do

Vinegar is often a tool rather than a star in the preserving process. Perhaps that is because the usual ones -- apple cider vinegar, white and red wine vinegar and malt vinegar -- don't often have any distinctive flavor to speak of. We have found that there is room to be incredibly experimental with vinegar when making colorful concoctions and seasonal preserves. Why not give it a try and become a vinegar chef? The flavored vinegars on these pages will keep for up to 1 year.

HOW TO MAKE RASPBERRY VINEGAR

Combine the vinegar, sugar and raspberries in a pan and simmer for 15 minutes on medium heat.

Strain the mixture through a fine sieve and pour into a sterilized bottle (see page 53).

HERB VINEGARS

Start by bruising your chosen herbs to release all their stored aromas. Bring 500 ml (2 cups) of apple cider vinegar to a gentle simmer in a pan and add the herbs. Turn off the heat and leave to cool, and then strain the vinegar into a sterilized bottle (see page 53).

FRUIT VINEGARS

Many fruits can be used to flavor vinegar. Use red wine vinegar for red fruits and white wine vinegar for lighter fruits. Bring 400 ml (1⅔ cups) of vinegar to a simmer in a pan then add 250g (9 ounces) fruit and 30–45 ml (2–3 tablespoons) of sugar. Bring back to a boil then turn off the heat and leave to cool. Scoop any scum off the top and strain the vinegar through a jelly bag or fine sieve into a sterilized bottle (see page 53).

FLORAL VINEGARS

You can also use flowers, such as lavender or nasturtiums, to make unusual vinegars. Use 500 ml (2 cups) white wine vinegar for 10–15 flower heads and prepare as for herb vinegars.

ROSE HIP VINEGAR

This flavored vinegar goes very well with chicken or fish, and can be drizzled over a melon and prosciutto salad for some added zing.

1 L (1¾ pints) apple cider vinegar

60 ml (¼ cup) sugar

50 g (2 ounces) rose hips

peel from 1 orange

Put the vinegar and sugar in a pan and heat until dissolved. Allow to cool then set aside. Meanwhile, thread the rose hips and pieces of orange peel alternately onto a wooden skewer. Place the skewer in a sterilized bottle (see page 53) and pour in the vinegar. Seal and leave for at least 2–3 weeks before using.

RASPBERRY VINEGAR

Delicious served with orange and red onion salad or as a dressing for a bulgur wheat and pomegranate salad, this simple vinegar is incredibly versatile. Try reducing it down to intensify the flavors.

400 ml (1⅔ cups) red wine vinegar

60 ml (¼ cup) sugar

250 g (9 ounces) raspberries

To make the raspberry vinegar, follow the instructions opposite.

For the ultimate in flavored vinegars, try this balsamic glaze -- a reduced balsamic vinegar that has been infused with the flavor of fresh figs.

Serves 4

200 g (7 ounces) fresh figs
300 ml (1¼ cups) balsamic vinegar
1 pinch ground cinnamon
1 pinch freshly grated nutmeg
3 juniper berries
15 ml (1 tablespoon) honey (optional)

FIG BALSAMIC GLAZE

Cut the figs into halves or quarters depending on their size, and then place them in a pan with all the other ingredients and heat until the vinegar starts to bubble. Reduce the heat and simmer for 15–20 minutes or until the vinegar has reduced to a third of its original volume. Finally, sieve the mixture through a funnel and into a sterilized glass or plastic bottle (see page 53). Store in the fridge.

Place the bottle of glaze in a bowl of warm water for 5 minutes before you want to use it. This will make it less viscous and easier to pour.

A perfect partnership

The oil is infused with flavor

PRESERVING IN OIL

Storing under a layer of oil is probably one of the oldest preserving techniques. It has the ability not only to keep garden produce fresh but also to create a delicious extra -- infused oils. Each jar will therefore provide you with two delicious opportunities: first you can consume the preserved contents as antipasto or use them as an ingredient in another dish, then the remaining infused oil can be used in salad dressings or for cooking.

PREPARING YOUR PRODUCE

If you are planning to preserve herbs or vegetables in oil, you will want the flavor to penetrate the golden liquid. Try to bruise herbs, toast nuts and crush seeds to release their flavor prior to storing. As much as possible, try to store dry produce rather than wet. Dry the herbs or vegetables with papertowels or in the oven before you place them in the container. The presence of water will reduce the keeping quality of the food.

PREPARING THE OIL

Different oils have very different flavors and qualities. Olive oil works fine, but try experimenting with others: canola and poppy seed for light dishes, walnut and hazelnut for crunchy flavor, peanut and sesame for Oriental cooking, and avocado for something a bit different.

Warming the basic oil first often helps it to absorb the flavor of the added ingredient more evenly, but you will be surprised at how easily flavor will leak into the oil molecules even if you use it cold.

PRESERVING

Put your prepared herbs or vegetables into sterilized jars or bottles (see page 53) and cover with oil. It's a good idea to use a funnel if you are filling a bottle. Ensure that you pack the container fully and, after the oil has been poured in, tap the bottom of the jar or bottle on a tea towel to dislodge any air bubbles. Seal and label.

Time is the key with oil preserving – always wait at least 3 days before using your oils, and wait longer for more intensity. Give the bottles a little shake during the first couple of days.

Keep the oil bottles and containers in a dark place to avoid discoloration. If you want to have your gorgeous oily collection on display, make sure it isn't in direct sunlight.

ROASTED PEPPERS IN OIL

First, cut your peppers into large slices. Put them on a baking sheet and drizzle with oil. Roast them in the oven at 180°C (350°F) for 45 minutes. Once the roasted peppers have cooled enough to handle, follow the numbered steps on this page. For added flavor when roasting the peppers, include some garlic cloves and put them into the jar with some bruised oily herbs, such as rosemary, thyme or oregano.

You can use exactly the same method to preserve eggplants, zucchini and artichokes.

Remove the skins, stalks and seeds from the roasted peppers. Tear or cut into slices and let dry on papertowels. Sprinkle with herbs.

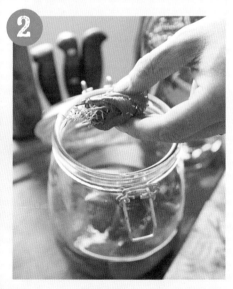

Place the prepared vegetables and any extra flavorings, such as herbs, in a sterilized jar (see page 53).

Fill the jar with olive oil, making sure that the vegetables are completely covered. Seal and store in the fridge or a cool, dark cupboard.

HERB OILS

Scented herb oils are a shortcut to masses of flavor and will preserve the aromatic qualities of any fresh herb for longer than dried herbs in jars. These are some of our favorite herb oils, but any fresh herbs will do.

MINT OIL

300 ml (1¼ cups) olive oil

5 ml (1 teaspoon) sugar

30 ml (2 tablespoons) chopped fresh mint

Put all the ingredients in a pan and heat for 10 minutes on medium heat. Leave to cool, then refrigerate for 1 hour. Mint tends to discolor over time, so strain through a fine sieve and store in a sterilized glass bottle (see page 53).

ROSEMARY & GARLIC OIL

4 garlic cloves, roasted

300 ml (½ pint) olive oil

3 large sprigs fresh rosemary

Roast the garlic in a preheated oven at 180°C (350°F) for 30 minutes. Ideally, do this when the oven is being used for something else. When the roasted garlic is cool, put it into a sterilized glass bottle (see page 53) with the oil and rosemary sprigs and leave to infuse for 2-3 days before using.

MIXED HERB OIL

2 sprigs fresh thyme

2 sprigs fresh oregano

2 sprigs fresh rosemary

6 fresh basil leaves

5 pink peppercorns

300 ml (1¼ cups) olive oil

Bruise the herb sprigs and basil leaves a little to release their flavor, and put them into a sterilized glass bottle (see page 53) with the peppercorns and olive oil. Leave to infuse for 2-3 days before using.

Flavored oil adds something special to goat cheese, but you can use the same method for any cheese with a similar texture and skin. This recipe turns the goat cheese into a meal in its own right. Just spread the cheese, oil, seeds and peppercorns on crisp bread or toasted whole-grain bread and enjoy.

Serves 4

150 g (5 ounces) soft or semi-soft goat cheese

15 ml (1 tablespoon) pink peppercorns

10 ml (2 teaspoons) fennel seeds

350 ml (1½ cups) good extra virgin olive oil

75 g (2½ ounces) olives, dried if they have been in brine (optional)

GOAT CHEESE WITH PINK PEPPERCORNS

Cut the goat cheese into large pieces – if you have small rounds with a skin on, cut them so that the inside of the cheese is exposed.

Heat the peppercorns and fennel seeds in a small, dry frying pan for a minute or two, removing them from the heat when they start giving off their aroma but before they are colored. Pour the oil into a bowl, add the warm fennel seeds and peppercorns and stir well.

Put the cheese carefully into a sterilized 500 ml (2-cup) jar (see page 53), trying not to crumble it, and adding the olives at the same time if you are using them. Tip the jar to one side and pour in the oil and spices. Make sure the oil covers the cheese – add more than listed if necessary. Put on the lid, then lay a folded tea towel on a work surface and tap the bottom of the jar on the towel to dislodge any air bubbles.

Store in a dark, cool cupboard for at least 24 hours before eating. The cheese will keep for up to 2 weeks unopened. Once opened, store in the fridge for up 10 days. Remove from the fridge 1 hour before you need it and serve at room temperature.

A small frying pan is ideal for dry-frying spices

METHOD #11

BOTTLING

Try bottling if you want rows of colorful jars lined up in your cupboard and a rich supply of fruit and vegetables ready to eat over the colder months. Bottling is a relatively simple preserving method and is worth attempting at home with your own home-grown goodies. Food is placed in jars with either a syrup for fruit or a brine for vegetables, and both the jars and the food are heated until all bacteria, mold, fungi and viruses are killed. The jars are then immediately sealed. It is very important that you invest in some good-quality jars as a good seal is required to prevent spoiling.

Make a hot brine solution (see opposite). Pack your jars as tightly as possible with skinned tomatoes, and then fill them with brine and place the lids on loosely.

Sterilize the filled jars (see opposite). After cooling, test for a good seal and vacuum by loosening the jar's clip or band and lifting the jar by the lid. If the seal does not hold, eat the contents quickly or freeze it or try again.

PREPARING CONTAINERS

You need some bottling jars, such as Mason jars, which are stronger than normal jam jars and have either tops or jars with clips and good rubber seals. Wash your jars thoroughly then sterilize them either in boiling water for 5 minutes or in the oven (see page 53).

PREPARING SYRUP & BRINE

For fruit, make a syrup with 400 g (14 ounces) of sugar (about 500 ml/2 cups) and 1 L (4 cups) of water and heat to over 60°C (140°F). Prepare the fruit by taking off stalks and stems, rinsing clean and coring or removing pits if you wish. For vegetables, make a brine with 25 g (1 ounce) of salt (about 30 ml/2 tablespoons) and 1 L (4 cups) of water. Prepare the vegetable as required.

STERILIZING BOTTLED FOOD

Pack the fruit into the jars and top up with the hot syrup. Carefully tap the jars on a work surface to force any air bubbles to the surface and help the fruit to settle. Having removed

SAFETY!

Acidity in food is important to prevent the botulinum bacteria from ruining your stored products, and to prevent serious, potentially fatal, food poisoning. For safety's sake, you need to heat the jars beyond the boiling point of water. With low-acid foods such as vegetables, this involves using a special canner, which is essentially a large pressure cooker designed for bottling.

any air gaps that could damage the fruit later, wet the rubber seals of the jars in boiling water and put them onto the lids of the jars. Seal the lids loosely and stand the jars on a wooden rack or a folded tea towel in a large pan. (If you are doing a lot of bottling it's worth investing in a special sterilizing pan with a false bottom for standing the jars on.) Pour in just enough cold water to reach the top of the jars, below the lids, place them on the stove and bring to a simmer according to the chart below.

BOTTLING GUIDELINES

SOFT FRUIT

Put the jars in cold water and raise the temperature slowly over the course of 1 hour to 60°C (140°F). Simmer at 80°C (175°F) for a further 10 minutes.

STONE FRUIT

Repeat as above for the first hour, but then heat the water up to 85°C (185°F) and keep at this temperature for 15 minutes.

TOMATOES & PICKLES

Repeat as above for the first hour, but then heat the water up to 90°C (195°F) and keep at this temperature for 30–40 minutes.

At the end of the summer there is a period when the new-season lambs have fattened and the chilies and figs have ripened. This dish brings together all these flavors and the mix of earthy, sweet and spice seems to us to perfectly sum up the end of summer.

Serves 4

1 red onion, cut into chunks
1 head of fennel, thinly sliced
½ a celery root, diced
1 sprig fresh rosemary
olive oil
800 g (1¾ pounds) lamb cutlets
salt and freshly ground black pepper
25 g (1 ounce) butter (about 30 ml/2 tablespoons)

For the figs in honey
6 large figs
150 ml (⅔ cup) honey

For the sauce
150 ml (⅔ cup) port
1 fresh red chili, seeded and chopped

To serve
mashed potatoes

HONEYED FIGS WITH LAMB

First, make the figs in honey. Simply place the fruit in a jar and pour over the honey. They will keep for 3–4 weeks.

Preheat the oven to 180°C (350°F). Place the onion, fennel and celery root in a roasting pan with the rosemary and a splash of olive oil. Bake for 30 minutes, then add 100 g (3½ ounces) of figs (about 2 or 3) to the roasting pan and put back into the oven for a further 10 minutes.

To make the sauce, slice 100 g (3½ ounces) figs (about 2 or 3) into small chunks and put them into a pan with the port and chili. Bring to a boil then reduce the heat and simmer until the sauce starts to thicken. Turn off the heat, sieve to remove the pieces of fig and chili and set the sauce to one side.

Season the lamb cutlets all over with salt and pepper. Melt the butter in a frying pan and fry the cutlets for 2–3 minutes on each side. Remove from the pan and keep warm.

Add a little honey from the jar of figs to the juices in the pan. Stir well, then whisk into the port sauce.

Arrange the cutlets, vegetables and figs on a serving platter and pour the sauce over then serve with mashed potoatoes.

Apricots preserved in almond-flavored **Amaretto** liqueur are delicious straight from the jar. **We** love them with rice pudding, but this recipe goes one step further to create a very special tart.

Serves 4

400 ml (1⅔ cups) milk

1 vanilla bean

100 g (3½ ounces) short grain rice

15 ml (1 tablespoon) crème fraîche or plain Greek-style yogurt, plus extra for serving

For the Amaretto apricots

10 apricots

250 ml (1 cup) Amaretto liqueur

For the pastry

125 g (4 ounces) softened butter

125 g (4 ounces) sugar

250 g (9 ounces) flour (about 500 ml/2 cups)

50 g (2 ounces) ground almonds (about 125 ml/ ½ cup)

For the topping

50 g (2 ounces) butter (about 45 ml/ 3 tablespoons), melted

30 ml (2 tablespoons) sugar

AMARETTO APRICOT TART

First make the Amaretto apricots. Halve the apricots and remove the pits, and then pack them gently into a sterilized jar (see page 53). Split the pits, put the kernels into the jar and top up with Amaretto. Store in a dark cupboard for at least 2 weeks before using. They will keep for up to 1 year.

To make the pastry, mix the butter and sugar in a bowl with a wooden spoon. Slowly add the flour and almonds, using your hands to bring the dough together into a ball. Wrap the dough in plastic wrap and store in the fridge while you make the filling.

Bring the milk to a boil, then add the vanilla bean and rice. Simmer on very low heat for 25 minutes.

While the rice is cooking, puree about 175 g (6 ounces) of the apricots to a smooth paste with a tablespoon of the liqueur. You need to reserve a few apricots for decoration. When the rice is cooked, remove the vanilla bean, then add the crème fraîche or yogurt and the apricot paste and stir thoroughly.

Preheat the oven to 200°C (400°F). Take the pastry out of the fridge and roll it out to fit a 25 cm (10-inch) flan pan. Prick the base with a fork then line with parchment paper and pastry weights or dry beans. Bake for 18–20 minutes, until a pale golden color. Remove the paper and weights and allow to cool.

Pour the rice filling into the cooked pastry. Drizzle with the butter and sugar then top with the remaining apricots. Cook in the oven for 20 minutes.

Serve warm, with a spoonful of crème fraîche or yogurt.

METHOD #12

RUMTOPF

Having lived in Germany, we thoroughly enjoy the traditional German Christmas treat of ice cream with rumtopf -- fruit preserved in rum. Rumtopf ("rum pot") allows you to eat out-of-season fruit all through the year and is particularly popular over the festive season. The fruit and liquid from a rumtopf are great with cream or ice cream, and you can add the liquid to sparkling wine to make a cocktail, or drink a small glass of it on its own. The content of a rumtopf is incredibly alcoholic -- you have been warned!

BEGINNING YOUR RUMTOPF

A rumtopf made in an authentic crock will give you up to 50 servings. If you can't find an authentic crock, you can use any lidded ovenproof pot with a volume of 2–3 L (2–3 quarts).

Clean the crock, dry it and start it off with 400 g (14 ounces) of any fruit except apples and 200 g (7 ounces) of sugar (about 250 ml/1 cup). Cover the fruit and sugar with rum, put plastic wrap over the rumtopf and put the lid on the pot.

ADDING TO YOUR RUMTOPF

Every time a new fruit comes into season, open the crock, put the fruit in, add more sugar and cover with rum again. We add 400 g (13 ounces) of each fruit at a time, plus half as much sugar, and continue adding fruit until the rumtopf is full. We usually start with strawberries, and then, as the seasons develop, we add cherries, plums, blackberries and raspberries. Once the last fruit has been added, leave undisturbed until Christmas.

FESTIVE RUMTOPF

For each addition to the crock:

400 g (14 ounces) of each type of soft fruit, whatever is in season (we use smallish strawberries, plums, cherries, blackberries and raspberries)

200 g (7 ounces) sugar (about 250 ml/1 cup) for each 400 g (14 ounces) fruit

strong brown rum, enough to cover the fruit (extra rum will be needed later in the year)

To preserve your fruit in the rumtopf, follow the instructions opposite.

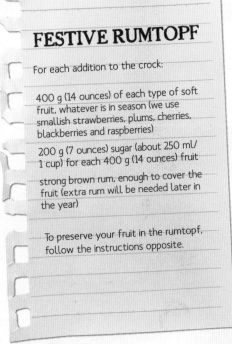

HOW TO MAKE A RUMTOPF

Add the fruit to the crock as each season arrives. Hull the strawberries, halve and pit the plums, pit the cherries and so on.

Put the fruit and sugar into the crock and cover with rum.

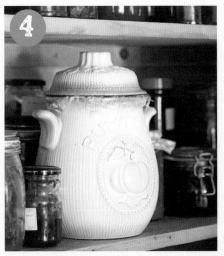

You need to keep the fruit underneath the liquid, so pop a plastic lid or saucer into the crock to hold them down.

Put plastic wrap over the top of the crock and put the lid on. Every time a new fruit comes into season, open the crock, put the fruit in, add more sugar and rum and cover again.

RELISHES

There is a thin line between a chutney and a relish. The cooking process is almost identical, and the textures are similar, but in our opinion there is a substantial difference in taste. If you make a relish, there is more scope for it to be sweeter, fruitier or have a potent mustard quality. Relishes are usually highly flavored, often spicy hot or sweet and sour. We find that a relish comes out of the cupboard with cheeses and whenever we eat homemade burgers.

PREPARING INGREDIENTS

As with many preserves, the first stage involves chopping your fruits and vegetables so they are ready for the process. With a relish, the general rule is to aim for small cubes that will spread nicely once cooked. If you put the chopped ingredients in a large glass bowl, you can see the quantities of the various ingredients. This will give you a good idea of the eventual taste and allows you to adjust the proportions as you like.

COOKING THE RELISH

Start by dissolving the sugar in the vinegar in a heavy-bottomed pan on medium heat. When it starts to simmer, add the fruits and vegetables and any spices. Bring to a boil, then return it to a simmer and cook for 30–45 minutes. When some of the vinegar starts to reduce and you are happy with the consistency, take the pan off the heat and pour the relish straight into sterilized jars (see page 53) – a funnel is useful here. A relish can be pulpy and set, more like a jam, or it can be juicy. If you want it to end up firm, make sure you cook it for longer.

FINISHING IT OFF

Near the end of the cooking process you can add some small ingredients, such as chopped pickles or pickled onions. This will improve the texture of your relish and give it a crunch and zingy flavor.

STORING YOUR RELISHES

Seal the jars right away and store them in a cool, dark place for up to 1 year. Once opened, keep refrigerated.

TOMATO RELISH

Makes 2 kg (4 pounds)

250 g (8 ounces) brown sugar

500 ml (2 cups) vinegar

1 kg (2 pounds) red tomatoes, finely chopped

150 g (5 ounces) onions, chopped

3 red chilies, chopped

30 ml (2 tablespoons) mustard seeds

5 ml (1 teaspoon) paprika

5 ml (1 teaspoon) ground ginger

salt and freshly ground black pepper

100 g (3½ ounces) pickles, finely chopped

100 g (3½ ounces) pickled onions, finely chopped

Put the sugar and vinegar in a large heavy-bottomed pan and heat until dissolved. Bring to a simmer and stir in the tomatoes, onions, chilies and spices. Cook over medium heat for 30 minutes then add the pickles and pickled onions. Simmer for a further 5 minutes then pour into sterilized jars (see page 53).

JALAPEÑO RELISH

Makes 1 kg (2 pounds)

125 g (4 ounces) light brown sugar (about 150 ml/²⁄₃ cup)

250 ml (1 cup) apple cider vinegar

500 g (1 pound) fresh jalapeño chilies, seeded and cut into 5 mm (¼-inch) strips

150 g (5 ounces) onions, cut into 5 mm (¼-inch) strips

150 g (5 ounces) carrots, cut into 5 mm (¼-inch) strips

5 ml (1 teaspoon) fennel seeds

5 ml (1 teaspoon) brown mustard seeds

5 ml (1 teaspoon) yellow mustard seeds

Put the sugar and vinegar in a large heavy-bottomed pan and heat gently until the sugar has dissolved. Put the chilies, carrot and onion into the vinegar solution and bring to a boil. Add the spices and simmer for 30 minutes then pour into sterilized jars (see page 53).

This corn relish is incredibly versatile, but we think it's especially good with pork, beans and a green salad. The further ahead you make the relish, the better, as storage improves the intensity of the flavors.

Serves 4

400 g (13 ounces) pork shoulder, diced
60 ml (¼ cup) honey
1 fresh red chili, seeded and chopped
5 ml (1 teaspoon) paprika
1 pinch cayenne pepper
30 ml (2 tablespoons) orange juice
5 ml (1 teaspoon) fennel seeds

For the sweetcorn and pepper relish
1 red onion, finely chopped
1 garlic clove, chopped
1-10 ml (2 teaspoons) sunflower oil

2 large cobs corn
1 red pepper, finely chopped
1 fresh red chili, seeded and finely chopped
juice of 1 lime
2 shots tequila
60 ml (¼ cup) white wine vinegar
100 g (3½ ounces) sugar (about 125ml/½ cup)
15 ml (1 tablespoon) chopped fresh cilantro

To serve
flatbread
refried beans
fresh salad leaves

SPICED PORK WITH CORN & PEPPER RELISH

First make the relish. Put the onion and garlic into a hot pan with the sunflower oil and soften without coloring on low heat. Slice the corn kernels off the cob with a sharp knife and add to the pan along with the pepper, chili and lime juice. Pour in the tequila and simmer for 2–3 minutes to burn off the alcohol, then add the vinegar and sugar. Heat for 10–15 minutes, stirring to prevent the mixture sticking to the base of the pan. Add the cilantro and pour into a sterilized jar (see page 53), Set aside until you are ready to serve. The relish will keep in the fridge for 4–6 weeks, but once opened, use within a week.

Put the pork into a bowl and add the rest of the ingredients. Leave to marinate for at least 1 hour. Meanwhile, soak eight wooden skewers in cold water.

Take the pork out of the marinade and cook it for 2–3 minutes on each side, either on skewers over a flame or in a griddle pan, brushing with the marinade during the cooking for extra stickiness.

Serve with flatbread, refried beans and a fresh green salad.

Cucumber and dill are a bit like tomato and basil -- their compatibility is unquestionable. Together they make a cooling relish that's perfect with a piece of fish.

Serves 4

100 g (3½ ounces) bread crumbs (about 175 ml/¾ cup)

15 ml (1 tablespoon) finely chopped fresh dill

zest of 1 lemon

5 ml (1 teaspoon) sea salt

freshly ground black pepper

30 ml (2 tablespoons) olive oil

4 (200 g/7-ounce) salmon fillets

For the relish

1 cucumber

30 ml (2 tablespoons) chopped fresh dill

15 ml (1 tablespoon) white wine vinegar

10 ml (2 teaspoons) sugar

5 ml (1 teaspoon) white mustard seeds (optional)

sea salt

For the vegetables

100 g (3½ ounces) cherry tomatoes

2 red peppers, cut into strips

olive oil

250 g (9 ounces) new potatoes, halved

20 g (¾ ounce) butter (about 22 ml/1½ tablespoons)

4 spring onions, finely chopped

250 g (9 ounces) green beans

salt and pepper

BAKED SALMON WITH CUCUMBER & DILL RELISH

Start by making the relish. Grate the cucumber into a pan and stir in the chopped dill. Add the vinegar, sugar and mustard seeds, if using, and stir over low heat for 5 minutes. Season with 1 pinch salt and set aside to cool. Stored in a sterilized jar (see page 53), the relish will keep in the fridge for up to 3 weeks.

Preheat the oven to 200°C (400°F). Put the bread crumbs in a bowl and add the dill, lemon zest, salt and pepper. Stir in the oil, then spread the mixture over the fish fillets and lay them on a baking sheet.

Put the tomatoes and peppers alongside the fish if there is room, otherwise use a separate pan. Drizzle with olive oil and sprinkle with salt and pepper, and then put the sheet(s) in the oven and cook for 20 minutes.

Meanwhile bring a large pan of water to a boil. Cook the potatoes for 15–20 minutes. When they're ready, drain and return them to the pan with the butter and the spring onions. Smash them up a bit with a fork. Blanch the green beans in boiling water for 3–4 minutes.

Serve the salmon fillets with the roasted vegetables, smashed potatoes, green beans and cucumber relish.

Duck and orange are renowned companions, since the acidity of the fruit cuts through the natural richness of the meat. This recipe adds vinegar and spices to the mix and makes a great accompaniment to cold duck or goose.

Makes 600 g (1¼ pounds)

5 large oranges
30 ml (2 tablespoons) extra virgin olive oil
1 large onion, chopped
2 Bramley apples, peeled and diced
seeds from 8 cardamom pods
5 ml (1 teaspoon) black mustard seeds
2 ml (½ teaspoon) ground cloves
150 g (5 ounces) light brown sugar (about 175 ml/¾ cup)
300 ml (1¼ cups) apple cider vinegar

SPICY ORANGE RELISH

Use a vegetable peeler to take off the zest of the oranges in pieces. Cut the zest into strips about 5 mm (¼ inch) wide and set aside. With a sharp knife, cut the pith and skin off the oranges and take out the flesh in segments.

Heat the oil in a pan then add the onion and cook until softened. Add the apples, cardamom and mustard seeds and cook for a further 5 minutes.

Add the orange segments and zest to the pan with the remaining ingredients and simmer for 40 minutes. Put into sterilized jars (see page 53) and allow to cool. Store the relish in the fridge, where it will keep for up to 6 months.

Serve with cold duck or goose, as a salad or in a sandwich.

You need segments without pith or peel

You have to try this

CHUTNEY

Chutney can be made from almost any fruit or vegetable. We've used marrows, runner beans, apples, radishes, rhubarb, red and green tomatoes, grapes, chilies, eggplant, squash, pears and turnips, to name but a few! The key when making chutney is to cook it for a long time and evaporate most of the moisture so that it reaches a thick, jam-like consistency. The colors will change, but the flavors will always intensify. The other thing to consider when cooking a good chutney is to be bold and contrast the flavors -- don't be afraid to mix fruits and vegetables.

CHOOSING FLAVORINGS

There are various spices that add those distinctive chutney flavors: cumin, coriander, allspice, cloves, ginger, peppercorns, paprika, mustard seed and garlic are some of the main ones. Crush your chosen spices with a pestle and mortar to release their aroma.

Vinegar is used in chutney because its acidity effectively inhibits the actions of unwanted microorganisms. Distilled vinegar is the strongest preservative but also one of the most expensive. The more you pay for your wine or malt vinegar, the tastier your chutneys will be. We tend to use a variety of different vinegars, including apple cider vinegar, white wine vinegar and red wine vinegar.

STORING

Most chutneys mature with age, and if kept in the right conditions will last for years. Once you have opened a jar of chutney, it will last longer if you keep it in the fridge.

GRANDPA'S RECIPE

Makes about 12 small jars

2.5 kg (5 pounds) green tomatoes, sliced

500 g (1 pound) onions, finely chopped

15 ml (1 tablespoon) salt

500 g (1 pound) cooking apples, peeled, cored and sliced

500 g (1 pound) golden raisins, chopped

1 L (4 cups) pickling vinegar

500 g (1 pound) light muscovado or dark brown sugar (about 625 ml/2½ cups)

5 small hot chilies, finely chopped

30 ml (2 tablespoons) ground ginger

Put the tomatoes and onions in a bowl, sprinkle with the salt and set aside for a few hours. Drain off the liquid and place the solids in a pan with the apple and golden raisins. Gently heat until the fruit softens. Add the vinegar, sugar, chilies and ginger and cook for at least 45 minutes. Pour into sterilized jars (see page 53) and seal.

HOW TO MAKE CHUTNEY

Start by slicing, dicing, peeling and coring all the fruits and vegetables you will be using. Then prepare the spice or herb mix.

Add the fruits, vegetables, herbs and spices to a pan and simmer until they start to soften.

Cook on medium to low heat for no less than 45 minutes. You will know when your chutney is ready because it will have reduced to a jam-like consistency and your kitchen will smell wonderful.

Remove the chutney from the heat and pour into sterilized jars (see page 53). Keep the jars in a cool, dark place and make sure that all the lids are securely sealed.

Chutney and cheese is a partnership that needs no introduction. Spicy chutneys are not to everyone's taste, but for those of us who enjoy a bit of heat, this preserve is hard to beat.

Serves 4

1 small baguette
1 garlic clove, crushed
30–45 ml (2–3 tablespoons) olive oil
300 g (10 ounces) goat cheese
200 g (7 ounces) mixed bitter salad leaves
1 carrot, grated

For the dressing
5 ml (1 teaspoon) lemon juice
15 ml (1 tablespoon) olive oil
5 ml (1 teaspoon) finely chopped fresh ginger
1 fresh red chili, seeded and finely chopped
5 ml (1 teaspoon) sesame seeds

For the chutney
3 fresh red chilies, chopped
2 large cooking apples, peeled, cored and chopped
450 g (15½ ounces) red tomatoes, chopped
2 red onions, finely chopped
200 g (7 ounces) sugar (about 250 ml/1 cup)
250 ml (1 cup) apple cider vinegar
100 g (3½ ounces) raisins, chopped
1 pinch cayenne pepper
1 pinch ground allspice
5 ml (1 teaspoon) chopped fresh ginger
salt and freshly ground black pepper

GOAT CHEESE CROSTINI WITH "SOME LIKE IT HOT" CHUTNEY

To make the chutney, put all the ingredients in a large pan, bring to a boil, then reduce the heat and simmer for 45 minutes. When the smells have filled your kitchen, the fruit has all softened and the vinegar has reduced, transfer the chutney into sterilized jars (see page 53) and store in a dark, cool place, where it will keep for 6–12 months. Allow the chutney to mature for 1 month before eating.

Slice the bread then toast it until golden. Rub a little crushed garlic and olive oil over one side of each piece of toast and spread some goat cheese on top.

Combine the bitter salad leaves and grated carrot in a bowl. To make the dressing, put the lemon juice, oil, ginger, chili and sesame seeds in a bowl and mix with a fork. Drizzle over the salad and serve with the crostini, topped with a dollop of chutney.

METHOD #15

JAMS & JELLIES

Jams and jellies are made in a similar way: both involve heating fruit with sugar to activate the pectin, a natural setting agent found in a variety of ripe fruits and vegetables, then storing it in a suitable container. Some fruits don't contain very much pectin, so you might need to add extra pectin, which you can buy, to some jams and jellies. What's the difference between a jam and a jelly? If there are any fruity bits in it, it's a jam. If not, it's a jelly.

GUIDELINES

- Always use undamaged fruit. Fruit that is damaged can spoil the flavor and the jam is likely to deteriorate quickly.
- If fruits are low in pectin, then either fruits with a higher level of pectin need to be included or pectin should be added.
- Always make sure the sugar is completely dissolved before bringing to a boil or the result can be grainy.
- Ensure all equipment you use is clean (for jelly-making, always boil-wash the cheesecloth, jelly bag or tea towel before using).
- Use a non-reactive pan (preferably stainless steel) and wooden or plastic spoons.
- Don't make too large a quantity at once or it can take a long time to come to a boil and the fruit can break up.
- Skim the scum that forms once the setting point has been reached.
- Allow the jam or jelly to stand for 15 minutes after a set has been reached before putting it into jars. This will aid the distribution of the fruit within the jars.

PECTIN GUIDELINES

FRUIT	PECTIN LEVEL
CITRUS PEEL	30%
ORANGES	0.5–3.5%
APPLES	1–1.5%
CARROTS	1.4%
APRICOTS	1%
CHERRIES	0.4%

- Store unopened jams and jellies in a cool, preferably dark place. Only store in the refrigerator once opened.

CHOOSING FRUITS

Not all fruits contain sufficient pectin to make jam or jelly successfully. Soft fruits, such as cherries, grapes and strawberries, contain small amounts of pectin, so to use them successfully you will need to add extra pectin to your recipe or use jam sugar (also called jelly sugar), which already has pectin in it. Apples, quinces, plums, gooseberries, blackberries, red currants, oranges and other citrus fruits contain large amounts of pectin.

MAKING JAM

Jams tend to be made with fruit that has been cut into pieces or crushed then heated with water and sugar. A good jam should have an even consistency – it should spread easily and have no free liquid.

MAKING JELLY

Jellies are clear or translucent fruit spreads and can be sweet, savory or spicy. The process for making a jelly is similar to that for making jam, but there is an additional step where the fruit pulp is strained out using a jelly bag.

A good jelly should quiver when moved but hold an angle when cut.

TESTING FOR SETTING POINT

Place a small plate in the fridge or freezer for 15 minutes. Pour a spoonful of the hot mixture onto the chilled plate and return it to the fridge for 5 minutes. To test, push the edge of the mixture with your index finger – it is ready when it wrinkles. If not, continue to cook, checking for setting point every few minutes. It is tempting to keep cooking to achieve a firmer set, but overcooking can be detrimental to the flavor.

STORING

All jams and jellies must be put into sterilized jars (see page 53) and sealed prior to storage. Jars with click-down lids (where the top of the lid bends inward as the air above the jam cools and contracts) are a good option as it is easy to tell if the seal has been maintained during storage. If the jam or jelly looks at all fizzy or moldy, the seal has failed.

Testing for setting

HOW TO MAKE STRAWBERRY JAM

Makes 3.25 kg (7 pounds)

2 kg (4 pounds) strawberries

2 kg (4 pounds) jam sugar (about 2.5 L/10 cups)

juice of 3 lemons

To make the strawberry jam, follow the numbered steps on this page and opposite.

Hull the strawberries and place them in a large non-reactive bowl (stainless steel, china or glass). Sprinkle over the sugar and lemon juice. Leave in the fridge overnight.

Turn off the heat and test for setting point (see page 93). If the jam is not setting, bring it back to a boil for 2 minutes and retest.

Once setting point has been reached, allow to cool for 5 minutes, then skim off any scum.

2

Put a small plate in the fridge to chill. Pour the contents of the bowl into a large, heavy-bottomed pan and heat gently until all the sugar has dissolved. Turn up the heat and boil vigorously for 5 minutes.

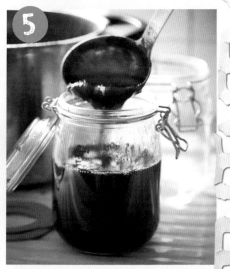

5

After a further 10 minutes, put the jam into sterilized jars (see page 53).

GOOSEBERRY JAM

Makes 5.5 kg (12 pounds)

2.5 kg (5 pounds) gooseberries

1 L (4 cups) water

3 kg (6½ pounds) jam sugar (about 3.75 L/
15 cups)

Put the gooseberries and water in a large, heavy-bottomed pan and gently heat until the fruit is soft. Add the sugar and heat until dissolved. Turn up the heat and boil rapidly for about 20 minutes or until the jam passes the test for setting point (see page 93). Skim off any skum and pour the jam into sterilized jars (see page 53).

APRICOT JAM

Makes 5 kg (11 pound)

2.5 kg (5 pounds) apricots

500 ml (2 cups) water

3 kg (6½ pounds) jam sugar (about 3.75 L/
15 cups)

Cut the apricots in half and remove the pits. Place the pits on a square of cheesecloth or in a jelly bag and tie into a bundle.

Put the apricots and water in a large, heavy-bottomed pan and gently heat until the fruit is tender. Add the sugar and heat until dissolved. Add the bag of apricot pits to the pan, turn up the heat and boil rapidly for about 25 minutes, until the jam passes the test for setting point (see page 93). When ready, pour the jam into sterilized jars (see page 53).

HOW TO MAKE ROSE PETAL JELLY

Makes 3.75 kg (8 pounds)

2 kg (4 pounds) Bramley apples

3 kg (6 pounds) sugar (about 3.75 L/15 cups)

4 drops edible rose essence

15 ml (1 tablespoon) dried edible rose petals

To make rose petal jelly, follow the numbered steps on this page and opposite.

Put a small plate in the fridge to chill. Cut up the apples, place them in a large pan and add just enough water to cover. Bring to a boil and simmer for 20 minutes.

Add 1kg (2 pounds) of sugar per 500 ml (2 cups) of apple liquid. Slowly bring to a boil, stirring to ensure the sugar dissolves. Boil for 5 minutes then cool for 3–4 minutes.

Skim off any scum. Boil again for 5 minutes, leave to cool for 3–4 minutes, then skim again. Test for setting point (see page 93). If not reached, boil for a further 5 minutes.

2

Strain the liquid through cheesecloth or a jelly bag. Don't squeeze the bag or you will end up with cloudy jelly. Measure the liquid and put it into a large, heavy-bottomed pan.

5

Add the rose essence and petals and stir in. When the jelly has cooled slightly, pour into sterilized jars (see page 53), adding a bit at a time to each jar. As the jars cool, rotate them to ensure that the petals do not sink or float.

RED CURRANT JELLY

Makes 2.75 kg (6 pounds)

3 kg (6 pounds) red currants

500 g (1 pound) jam sugar (about 625 ml/2½ cups) per 500 ml (2 cups) juice

Put a small plate in the fridge to chill. Place the red currants in an unsealed glass jar. Place the jar in a pan of cold water and bring to a simmer over low heat. Simmer for about 1 hour, mashing the berries from time to time.

Strain the fruit through cheesecloth or a jelly bag, allowing it to drain overnight. Measure the liquid and put it into a large, heavy-bottomed pan. Add 500 g (1 pound) of preserving sugar per 500 ml (2 cups) red currant juice.

Turn up the heat and boil for 5 minutes. Test for setting point (see page 93). When ready, skim off any scum and pour the jam into sterilized jars (see page 53).

Cream teas are an English ritual that just about everyone should be familiar with. That said, the big debate is whether you put the jam or the cream on the scone first. For us it doesn't really matter, as long as there is plenty of both!

Makes 10–12

450 g (14½ ounces) self-rising flour

1 ml (¼ teaspoon) salt

100 g (3½ ounces) unsalted butter (about 105 ml/ 7 tablespoons), cut into small cubes

75 g (3 ounces) superfine sugar (about 150 ml/ ⅔ cup)

250 ml (1 cup) buttermilk

10 ml (2 teaspoons) vanilla extract

1 egg, beaten

30 ml (2 tablespoons) milk

To serve

clotted cream

strawberry jam

THE ULTIMATE CREAM TEA

Preheat the oven to 220°C (425°F). Grease and flour a baking sheet, or use a silicone baking mat.

Place the flour, salt, butter and sugar in a large bowl and rub together with your fingertips until all the butter has been incorporated. In a smaller bowl or a jug, combine the buttermilk, vanilla and most of the egg. Gradually pour the buttermilk mixture into the large bowl, mixing gently with your hand. It's important not to overmix as that will knock the air out of it.

Turn the mixture out onto a work surface and shape it into a circle about 4 cm (1¾ inches) thick. Using a cutter about 6 cm (2½ inches) in diameter, stamp out circles and place them on the prepared baking sheet. Mix the milk with the remaining egg and use this to glaze the top of the scones.

Bake for about 15 minutes, until risen and golden brown. When ready, transfer them to a rack for about 10 minutes. Slice in half, spread with plenty of cream and jam and enjoy with a cup of tea.

For a really fancy-looking fruit tart, apricot jam is essential. It glazes the fruit -- keeping it moist and bright -- and flavors the pastry while also preventing sogginess or drying.

Serves 4

For the pastry

50 g (2 ounces) sugar (about 60 ml/¼ cup)

100 g (3½ ounces) butter (about 105 ml/ 7 tablespoons), softened

1 egg, beaten

200 g (7 ounces) flour (about 400 ml/1⅔ cups)

1 pinch salt

For the apricot glaze

100 g (3½ ounces) apricot jam

15 ml (1 tablespoon) water

15 ml (1 tablespoon) Grand Marnier liqueur

For the custard

50 g (2 ounces) sugar (about 60 ml/¼ cup)

3 large egg yolks

20 g (¾ ounce) flour (about 37 ml/2½ tablespoons)

20 g (¾ ounce) cornstarch (about 30 ml/ 2 tablespoons)

300 ml (1¼ cups) milk

5 ml (1 teaspoon) vanilla extract

For the fruit

100 g (3½ ounces) blackberries

100 g (3½ ounces) raspberries

100 g (3½ ounces) strawberries, sliced

1 kiwi fruit, sliced

TUTTI-FRUTTI TART

To make the pastry, beat the sugar and softened butter together in a bowl and gradually add the egg, flour and salt. Form into a ball, wrap in plastic wrap, and put in the fridge for 30 minutes.

Meanwhile, make the apricot glaze. Heat the apricot jam, water and Grand Marnier in a saucepan until smooth, and then strain through a fine sieve to remove any lumps. Leave to cool while you make the custard.

Mix the sugar and egg yolks together in a bowl, and then sift in the flour and cornstarch. Stir until you have a smooth paste. Heat the milk in a pan with the vanilla until it just starts to boil, and then remove from the heat and add it gradually to the flour mixture, stirring slowly. When all the milk is incorporated, pour it back into the pan and return it to the heat for another few minutes, whisking constantly until the custard comes to a boil and thickens. Turn off the heat, cover and set aside to cool.

Preheat the oven to 180°C (350°F), and grease a 20 cm (8-inch) cake pan. Take the pastry out of the fridge and roll it out to fit the pan. Lay the pastry in the pan, prick the base with a fork and then line with parchment paper and pastry weights or dried beans. Bake for 12–15 minutes then remove the paper and weights. Allow to cool.

Brush inside the pastry case with some of the glaze and allow it to dry. Pour in the cooled custard. Arrange the fruit on top in overlapping concentric circles. Warm the rest of the glaze and brush over the fruit.

This is a delicious way to serve game meat. Wrapping it in sausage meat helps it stay moist, so tender game that usually suffers from drying out, such as pigeon, pheasant and rabbit, can be used in this little roast.

Serves 4

8 slices air-dried ham

500 g (1 pound) venison sausage meat

500 g (1 pound) tender game meat (e.g. 2 pigeon breasts, 1 pheasant breast, 2 rabbit loin fillets)

8 tablespoons red currant jelly (see page 97)

½ a shallot, finely diced

250 ml (1 cup) port

50 g (2 ounces) butter (about 45 ml/3 tablespoons)

POACHER'S SUPPER WITH RED CURRANT SAUCE

Preheat the oven to 180°C (350°F).

Lay two slices of ham on a work surface so that they slightly overlap, trimming off the edges to form a square. Do the same with the rest of the ham slices. Divide the sausage meat into four portions, flatten them out and lay one portion on each square of ham. Cut your game meat into strips about 5 mm (¼ inch) thick and arrange them along the center of the sausage meat at right angles to the overlap in the ham slices.

Spread about 15 ml (1 tablespoon) of red currant jelly over the meat and roll up each square of ham so you have game and jelly surrounded by sausage meat and wrapped in ham. Secure the rolls with toothpicks, place them on a baking sheet and bake for 20 minutes then let rest for 5 minutes.

While the meat is cooking, make the sauce. Simmer the shallot in the port until reduced and sticky. Stir in about 60 ml (¼ cup) of red currant jelly and, when it is heated through, take it off the heat and stir in the butter.

Cut the meat into disks and serve with the sauce poured over. Root vegetables and mashed potatoes are good accompaniments.

Be generous with the jelly

A savory jelly not only adds flavor to a dish, it will also contrast nicely with the other textures. This recipe transforms fresh rosemary into the star of the dish instead of just the background flavor.

Serves 4

20 g (¾ ounce) butter (about 22 ml/1½ tablespoons)

350 g (2½ ounces) oyster mushrooms, sliced

1 sprig fresh rosemary

2 garlic cloves, chopped

5 ml (1 teaspoon) lemon juice

100 ml (3½ ounces) sherry

100 ml (3½ ounces) chicken stock

salt and freshly ground black pepper

2 balls mozzarella cheese

For the rosemary jelly

2 large sprigs of fresh rosemary

250 g (9 ounces) cooking apples, chopped

100 ml (scant ½ cup) water

1 garlic clove (optional)

100 ml (scant ½ cup) white wine vinegar

30 ml (2 tablespoons) sugar

30 ml (2 tablespoons) chopped fresh rosemary

MOZZARELLA & MUSHROOMS WITH ROSEMARY JELLY

Start by making the jelly. Put the rosemary sprigs, chopped apples and water in a pan and cook over low heat for 30 minutes – you can add a clove of garlic at this point if you like. Add the vinegar, bring to a rolling boil for 5 minutes, and then spoon the mixture into a jelly bag suspended over a bowl and leave for a few hours or overnight.

Put a small plate in the fridge to chill. When all the liquid has dripped through the bag, put it in a pan with the sugar and chopped rosemary. Place on a high heat for 5 minutes, or until setting point is reached (see page 93). Skim off any scum and pour the mixture into sterilized jam jars (see page 53) and place them in the fridge for 5–10 minutes, removing them before the jelly fully sets. Cover and return to the fridge for a further hour, until set.

Melt the butter in a pan, toss in the mushrooms with the rosemary, garlic and lemon juice, and cook for 5 minutes. Add the sherry and let the mushrooms cook until the alcohol has evaporated. Remove the mushrooms from the pan and divide between four plates.

Add the chicken stock to the mushroom juices and reduce the liquid for a couple of minutes on a high heat. Season with salt and pepper, then strain the sauce and pour around the mushrooms.

Set half a mozzarella ball on each plate and top with a spoonful of jelly.

A classic trifle contains sponge fingers, sherry, fruit, jelly, custard and cream. This version takes trifle to another level. It may seem that there is only a thin layer of jelly, but the flavor is there in abundance.

Serves 8-10

½ a package of sponge fingers

125 g (4 ounces) amaretti cookies

150 ml (⅔ cup) sherry

450 g (15½ ounces) fresh strawberries

75 g (3 ounces) toasted almond flakes

500 ml (2 cups) custard

For the strawberry and champagne jelly

1 kg (2 pounds) strawberries, hulled and quartered

250 ml (1 cup) champagne

1 kg (2 pounds) jam sugar (about 1.25 L/5 cups), or 1 kg (2 pounds) granulated sugar (about 1.25 L/5 cups) plus 15 ml (1 tablespoon) fruit pectin

For the topping

450 ml (1¾ cups) heavy cream (36%)

50 g (2 ounces) superfine sugar (about 60 ml/¼ cup)

125 ml (½ cup) champagne

STRAWBERRY & CHAMPAGNE TRIFLE

First make the jelly. Put a small plate in the fridge to chill. Place the strawberries and champagne in a large pan and heat until the fruit is soft and the total volume has reduced by about one-third. Add the sugar and stir until it has dissolved, then simmer for about 20 minutes, until setting point is reached (see page 93). If necessary, simmer for a bit longer. When the jelly is ready, strain it through a jelly bag into sterilized jars (see page 53) and keep in the fridge for up to 3 months.

Line a glass bowl with the sponge fingers and amaretti cookies and sprinkle them with the sherry. Warm 150–250 g (5–8 ounces) of jelly in a small pan until it's runny then pour it over the cookies. Arrange the fruit and all but a small handful of almonds on top of the jelly, then pour the cold custard over.

To make the topping, whip the cream and sugar to soft peaks, then gently fold in the champagne. Spoon over the custard and sprinkle the remaining almonds on top.

Pour jelly over the cookies

Making jelly from crab apples is a big treat. In fact, we'd go so far as to say that crab apple jelly is probably one of the best-kept secrets in the preserving world. We use it with game as a substitute for red currant jelly.

Serves 2-4

5 ml (1 teaspoon) chopped fresh thyme

5 ml (1 teaspoon) chopped fresh parsley

250 g (9 ounces) sausage meat

zest of 1 lemon

75 g (2½ ounces) apricots, chopped

150 g (5 ounces) chestnuts, chopped

1 large pheasant, boned

75 g (2½ ounces) butter (about 75 ml/⅓ cup)

4 slices bacon

15 ml (1 tablespoon) flour

150 ml (⅔ cup) chicken stock

salt and freshly ground black pepper

For the crab apple jelly

2 kg (4 pounds) crab apples

500 g (1 pound) sugar (about 625 ml/2½ cups)

juice of 1 lemon

To serve

peas

roasted vegetables

STUFFED PHEASANT WITH CRAB APPLE JELLY

First make the jelly. Put a small plate in the fridge to chill. Place the fruit in a saucepan and cover with water. Bring to a boil then simmer for 30 minutes, until the fruit starts to soften. Strain through a jelly bag for a few hours or overnight. When all the liquid has dripped through the bag, put it in a pan with the sugar and lemon juice and place on medium heat. Bring to a boil then simmer for about 45 minutes. Check for setting point (see page 93) then skim off any scum. Pour the jelly into sterilized jars (see page 53), seal and refrigerate. It will keep for 2–3 months.

Preheat the oven to 200°C (400°F). Put the herbs, sausage meat, lemon zest, apricots and chestnuts in a bowl and mix together. Stuff your pheasant with the mixture and put it in a roasting pan on a rack. Smear the butter over the bird and cover the breast with the bacon. Roast for 45 minutes then transfer the bird to a serving plate to keep warm.

Stir the flour into the pheasant juices in the tray, and then mix in the stock and 30 ml (2 tablespoons) of the crab apple jelly. Place on high heat for 2–3 minutes, stirring constantly with a whisk. Season the sauce with salt and pepper.

Serve the pheasant with peas, roasted vegetables and the sauce.

METHOD #16

MARMALADES

There is nothing quite like homemade marmalade. Traditionally, Seville oranges are used, as they are bitter and, when combined with sugar, give a really intense orangey flavor. That said, the season for Seville oranges is short, so it makes sense either to make your year's supply then or to freeze the oranges and use them at your convenience. Of course, it is possible to make a really interesting marmalade all year round using any combination of store-bought citrus fruits. Lemons and limes are definitely worth trying, but be prepared to simmer lemon and lime peel for a lot longer than orange peel to soften it -- up to 90 minutes.

HOW TO MAKE MARMALADE

Makes 2.25 kg (5 pounds)

1.5 kg (3 pounds) Seville oranges

2 lemons

500 ml (2 cups) water

2 kg (4 pounds) sugar (about 2.5 L/ 10 cups)

To make the marmalade, follow the numbered steps on this page and opposite.

First, scrub the oranges. Peel them, using a potato peeler or a sharp knife, and cut the peel into fine strips. Place a sieve over a large bowl and squeeze as much juice as possible out of the oranges and one of the lemons.

Keep all the skin, pith, pits and flesh from the sieve and place them, along with the peel and pith from both lemons, on a square of cheesecloth or in a jelly bag, and tie into a bundle. Put a small plate in the fridge to chill.

Put the orange peel, juice and water in a large stainless-steel pan and hang the bag of bits in it. Bring to a boil and simmer for 30 minutes, uncovered, until the peel is soft. Remove the bag and place it on a plate to cool.

When it is cool enough to handle, squeeze as much as you can out through the cheesecloth and into the pan. Add the sugar and stir until dissolved. At this stage you can taste and add more sugar if necessary.

Put the pan of marmalade on medium heat and allow it to boil rapidly for 15 minutes. Skim off any scum. Test for setting point (see page 93). When ready, pour into sterilized jars (see page 53) then seal and store.

Marmalade can be used for a lot more than just spreading on your toast. The bitterness of the orange rind cuts through the richness of the bread pudding beautifully, but you can make this dish with any citrus marmalade. While this pudding is gorgeous on its own, you can pour some heavy cream over it if you fancy.

Serves 6

8 slices of brioche loaf, crusts removed

50 g (2 ounces) softened butter (about 45 ml/3 tablespoons)

125 ml (½ cup) orange marmalade

3 eggs

60 ml (¼ cup) superfine sugar

5 ml (1 teaspoon) vanilla extract

500 ml (2 cups) light cream (20%)

30 ml (2 tablespoons) whiskey

MARMALADE BREAD PUDDING

Preheat the oven to 160°C (325°F).

Butter the slices of brioche and make four sandwiches, each filled with at least 15 ml (1 tablespoon) of marmalade. Cut the sandwiches into triangles and butter the outsides, and then lay them in rows in a suitably sized baking dish.

Beat the eggs in a bowl and add the sugar, vanilla, cream and whisky. Beat again then pour over the brioche sandwiches. Allow to stand for at least 20 minutes then use the remaining marmalade to make little orangey blobs all over the pudding.

Bake for about 45 minutes, until golden. Cool for 5 minutes before serving.

Who needs candies?

CANDIED PEEL

This method creates perhaps the prettiest of our preserved treats. Candied citrus peel is colorful, sweet and perfect for decorating cakes -- and the process is surprisingly easy. The important thing is to make sure the fruit you use is wax-free. Here we have candied the peel of grapefruit, oranges, limes and lemons. Other fruit, such as cherries and pineapple, will crystallize in a similar way to the peel. Follow the same method of cooking in a syrup, then another increasingly strong syrup and finally making sure that they are dry. Experiment and have fun -- you'll be well rewarded.

HOW TO MAKE CANDIED PEEL

Start by preparing the peel of your chosen citrus fruit. Use a very sharp knife to score a cross around the fruit then carefully remove the peel.

Place the peel in a pan with enough water to cover it and heat gently for 1 hour. Try to change the water a few times during the cooking, if you can, to remove any scum.

Strain, then use a teaspoon to remove the pith from inside the peel. This is the time either to cut the peel into strips or leave it as larger rustic pieces.

Weigh the peel then return it to the pan and add the same weight of sugar. Add a little water, enough to dissolve the sugar, and place on a low heat for 45 minutes. Repeat the process with a second batch of syrup.

Lay the peel on a baking sheet and leave to cool. Alternatively, you can place the tray in the oven at 80°C (175°F) for 1 hour. Dip the dried peel in superfine sugar and store in a sterilized jar (see page 53).

CHOCOLATE-DIPPED CANDIED PEEL

1 pink grapefruit

2 oranges

2 limes

1 lemon

Follow the numbered steps opposite and on this page, but when the peel is ready, melt some chocolate in a bowl over simmering water and dip half of each piece of candied peel into the sweet molten coating. Place on a rack or sheet of parchment paper to set.

METHOD #18

FRUIT CURDS

A fruit curd is a dessert spread usually made with the juice and zest of citrus fruit (though other fruits can also be used), combined with egg yolks, sugar and sometimes butter. When the spread is cold it is a smooth and very flavorful alternative to jam. It's lovely simply served on scones or fresh bread, but homemade fruit curds also make amazing fillings for tarts, cakes and the classic lemon meringue pie.

PREPARING THE FRUIT

Chilled citrus fruits are easier to grate or zest, but the zest dries out quickly, so cover it with plastic wrap until you need it. Room-temperature citrus fruits will yield more juice – roll them on a work surface prior to squeezing to get the maximum amount of juice out of them.

MAKING THE CURD

There are two ways to make fruit curd: you can add the butter to the eggs (see below) or vice versa (see numbered steps opposite). Both methods work equally well.

Put the eggs, sugar, zest and juice into a heatproof bowl and whisk until well combined. Place the bowl over a pan of simmering water, making sure the water does not touch the bottom of the bowl, and stir continuously until the mixture becomes thick. Remove from the heat. If you want perfectly smooth curd, pass the mixture through a sieve to remove the zest. Stir in the butter. Pour into a sterilized jar (see page 53) and seal immediately. Keep in the fridge.

STORING

As fresh eggs are used, these fruit curds do not keep as long as jams and therefore tend to be made in relatively small batches. Fruit curd will keep for about 4 weeks in the fridge.

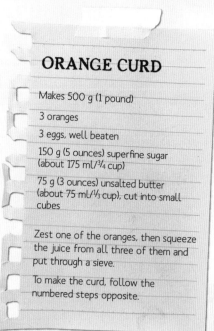

ORANGE CURD

Makes 500 g (1 pound)

3 oranges

3 eggs, well beaten

150 g (5 ounces) superfine sugar (about 175 mL/¾ cup)

75 g (3 ounces) unsalted butter (about 75 mL/⅓ cup), cut into small cubes

Zest one of the oranges, then squeeze the juice from all three of them and put through a sieve.

To make the curd, follow the numbered steps opposite.

HOW TO MAKE LEMON CURD

Makes 600g (1¼ pounds)

4 lemons

100 g (3½ ounces) butter
(about 105 ml/7 tablespoons)

450 g (14½ ounces) sugar
(about 560 ml/2¼ cups)

4 large eggs, beaten

Zest the lemons then squeeze the
juice from them and put through a
sieve.

To make the curd, follow the
numbered steps on this page.

Put the lemon zest and juice, butter and sugar
in a heatproof bowl over a pan of simmering
water. Gradually heat, whisking until the
butter melts then take off the heat.

Beat the eggs well and gradually drizzle them
into the lemon mixture, whisking all the time.
Return to the heat and continue to whisk as
the mixture heats up.

Cook for about 10 minutes, until the curd
thickens, then pour into sterilized jars
(see page 53). Seal and, when cool, store
in the fridge.

This sharp-flavored cake has an underlying sweetness. Feel free to make two cakes and sandwich them with lemon curd for a seriously tangy surprise.

Serves 8

confectioners' sugar, for dusting

30 ml (2 tablespoons) lemon curd

100 g (3½ ounces) superfine sugar (about 125 ml/½ cup)

100 g (3½ ounces) unsalted butter, softened (about 105 ml/7 tablespoons)

150 g (5 ounces) self-rising flour (about 310 ml/1¼ cups)

2 large eggs (at room temperature), beaten

zest of 1 lemon

For the lemon drizzle

juice of 2 lemons

50 g (2 ounces) superfine sugar (about 60 ml/¼ cu

To serve

crème fraîche, or plain Greek-style yogurt

lemon curd (see page 117)

LEMON CURD CAKE

Preheat the oven to 170°C (325°F). Grease a shallow 20 cm (8-inch) cake pan and dust it with confectioners' sugar.

Beat the lemon curd, sugar and butter in a large bowl. Sift in the flour while continuing to beat. Add the eggs and beat again, and finally add the lemon zest.

Pour the mixture into the cake pan and bake for 35 minutes, and then allow to cool in the pan for 10 minutes, until the cake shrinks slightly away from the sides. Transfer to a wire rack and leave to cool.

Mix the lemon drizzle ingredients together and drizzle over the cooled cake.

Serve slices of the cake with a spoonful each of crème fraîche or yogurt and lemon curd.

You have to try this

FRUIT CHEESES

Fruit cheeses are made from a stiff fruit puree and are a great way of preserving fruit that has a lot of seeds or pits as the pulp is passed through a sieve. The method works best with fruits that have a high pectin level (see pages 92–93). The basic process is simple: equal amounts of fruit pulp and sugar are heated gently for about 1 hour, until the sugar has dissolved and the mixture has thickened. Fruit cheeses are often spreadable and go really well with cheese and cold meats. They should be left for up to 2 months to mature and will keep for 4 months if stored in a sealed jar.

MEMBRILLO – QUINCE CHEESE

This is far and away our favorite fruit cheese. *Membrillo* is the Spanish word for "quince," and in Spain they have been making a cheese with it in a similar fashion for hundreds of years. The golden fruits make a delicious sweet condiment. Quinces are particularly high in pectin, so they set very well, and the gorgeous coral pink color looks great on a cheese board!

Makes 750 g (1½ pounds)

1.5 kg (3 pounds) quinces

1 vanilla bean

superfine sugar

Peel and core the quinces, and then cut them into pieces and put in a large pan. Cover them with water and add the vanilla bean. Put a lid on the pan and boil for 40 minutes. When all the quince pieces are soft, remove from the pan with a slotted spoon and place in a bowl. Discard the quince syrup.

Weigh the quince pulp and return it to the pan. Add an equal weight of sugar and place on low heat, stirring gently until the sugar dissolves. Keep cooking for a further hour, until the quinces have thickened into a rich coral pink paste.

Preheat the oven to 50°C (120°F). Grease a baking sheet and line it with parchment paper. Pour the paste into the prepared pan and smooth it out to the edges. Bake for 1 hour — this will help the cheese to set more quickly. When cool, slice into small portions and store in the fridge.

HOW TO MAKE A FRUIT CHEESE

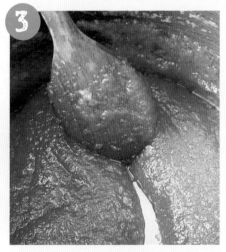

Chop your chosen fruit, place it in a large, thick-bottomed pan and cover with water. Bring to a boil then reduce the heat and simmer for 30–40 minutes or until the fruit has softened.

Strain the liquid out of the fruit, and then weigh the pulp. Put the pulp back into the pan and add the same weight of sugar. Place on low heat and stir until the sugar has dissolved.

Continue to stir for 1 hour, still over low heat, until the pulp thickens. To test for readiness, drag a spoon through the mixture: if it leaves a visible line, it is good to store.

Pour the fruit cheese into a mold (or small bowls greased with glycerine if you like, so it's easy to serve later) and cover the surface with a circle of parchment paper. Leave for a week to mature before enjoying.

4

BOTTLES

INTRODUCTION TO

BOTTLES

Bottling is a very versatile preserving technique and shows off the breadth of products that can be made at home beautifully. You can bottle everything from refreshing homemade beer or cider to herbal tinctures that can help relieve minor ailments such as coughs, colds or indigestion. Vegetable ketchups and fruit cordials or concentrates, made when the ingredients are plentiful and at their best, can preserve those fleeting, seasonal flavors for enjoyment throughout the year. The only thing these diverse products have in common is that they are stored in bottles with sealable stoppers, but all of them will make useful -- and very decorative -- additions to your kitchen and cupboard shelves.

GUIDELINES

• Make sure your bottles and any other pieces of equipment you use are clean – wash them with boiling water or use cleaning and sterilizing solutions.
• The seals on the bottle tops must be in good condition. For flip tops this is easy to confirm, but when reusing older bottles, you must make a proper inspection.
• Always label your bottle with the product it contains, the date of bottling and any other notes (if you have deviated from the recipe, for example).

CORDIALS

One old dictionary definition of a cordial is "a comforting or pleasant-tasting medicine." These days a cordial is generally not something medicinal but a sweet, non-alcoholic, usually fruit-flavored viscous liquid that is diluted with water to make a refreshing drink, like a concentrate. Our cordials are created with the best-quality fruits to produce a drink that can be enjoyed by all the family. It is worth remembering that there is more to

these soft drinks than just adding water and ice: you can try adding them to hot water or apple juice and infusing them with spices to make a deliciously warming drink, perfect on a cold winter's evening. Or in the summer, you could serve chilled dry white wine with a dash of fruit cordial for a fine aperitif. Raspberry, blackberry or peach concentrates are particularly good served in this manner.

WINES & CIDERS

The natural yeasts and sugars that are present in fruits and vegetables should be celebrated, and the person who discovered, thousands of years ago, that yeast turns those sugars into alcohol and carbon dioxide did us all a huge favor. It is extremely easy to make your own alcoholic drinks, be it wine, cider or even something a little stronger, though it must be said that it is more of an issue to make them well. You might not produce an exceptional wine your first time around, but those early attempts are special, so enjoy every glass. Start with a small batch, take careful notes about what you do and how you like the results, and

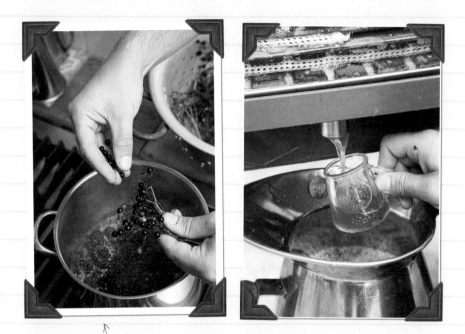

Remove the berries by hand or use a fork

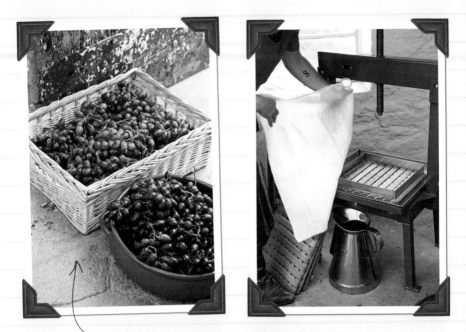

Collect ripe grapes on a dry day and juice them as soon as possible refine the process when you try again. When it comes to making wine, most people will immediately think of grapes, but you can make wine from almost anything – rose hips, nettles, parsnips or even pea pods.

Over recent years we have been making more cider, as there is an abundance of apples in our neighborhood. It is quite a task, and we tend to get friends together so that all can share in the fun and the spoils. Some of our cider has been very potent, so we are quite careful not to drink too much. Our first batch of cider (about 90 L/24 gallons) was extremely dry, so we turned it into spiced cider by adding lots of spices and sugar. Delicious!

SAUCES & KETCHUPS

A dash of hot homemade chili sauce or a dollop of creamed horseradish will liven up many a dish, and it's always good to have a bottle of fresh pesto on stand-by in the fridge for a quick weeknight supper. Ketchups are sweet, tangy condiments typically made with vegetables, vinegar, sugar and spices. Tomato ketchup is probably the most popular variety available today, but many other versions exist, from anchovy- and mushroom-based sauces to the banana ketchup popular in the Philippines.

TO MAKE TOMATO KETCHUP

Each brand of tomato ketchup has its own distinctive flavor, so when you make it at home you can expect to produce your own unique variation. Tomato ketchup is nothing new – the recipe below dates back more than 200 years and is quite salty because salt acts as a preservative.

• Harvest ripe tomatoes on a dry day and squeeze them into a pulp with your hands.
• Add 500 g (1 pound) of salt (about 500 ml/2 cups) per 100 tomatoes and boil for 2 hours, stirring occasionally to prevent the tomatoes from burning.
• Pass the tomatoes through a fine sieve to remove the skin and seeds.
• Add mace, nutmeg, allspice, cloves, cinnamon, ginger and pepper to taste.
• Boil slowly until the sauce is thick.
• Pour into sterilized bottles (see page 53). Apparently, this ketchup would keep for 2 or 3 years, but then again, they did not have expiry dates 200 years ago.

TINCTURES

A tincture is an herbal extract. The active ingredients of herbs and other plants are dissolved in alcohol – vodka works very well – or in a mixture of alcohol and water. All over the world, herbs have long been prized for their medicinal qualities as well as for their flavors. Purple coneflower – also known as echinacea – is believed to stimulate the immune system, relieve pain and reduce inflammation and was used by Native Americans for hundreds of years. Chamomile, valerian and lavender are all thought to have a calming effect and are used as remedies for sleep disorders and anxiety; peppermint will soothe an upset stomach and aid digestion; and elderberry extract is used to treat coughs and colds.

The very act of soaking herbs, or combinations of herbs, in alcohol and pressing the goodness out of them can feel therapeutic in itself. In fact, making tinctures can encourage you to take some responsibility for looking after yourself. That said, we are not advocating these tinctures as alternatives to conventional medicine, just something to complement it. Not all tinctures are safe for oral consumption, so make sure to do your research first.

CORDIALS

If you are looking for a way to preserve fruit flavors, making your own cordials is a very good move. Not only do they retain lots of flavor, but they also keep fresh in sealed bottles for a year. We use cordials diluted with water as a refreshing drink or in alcoholic drinks as a fancy mixer. Another great use for cordials is to drizzle them over fruit salad or ripple them through ice cream. Mint, lime, orange and pomegranate are some of our favorites.

MAKING CORDIALS

To make a cordial you need to simmer your fruit with some water to extract all the flavor. Once the fruit has softened, strain and measure the liquid before returning it to the pan and adding 350 g (11½ ounces) of sugar (425 ml / 1¾ cups) per 500 ml (2 cups) of juice. Put over low heat until the sugar has dissolved, then pour into sterilized bottles (see page 53) and seal.

ELDERFLOWER CORDIAL

Makes 1 L (4 cups)

1.5 kg (3 pounds) sugar (1,875 ml/8 cups)

15 elderflower heads, shaken to remove any insects

2 lemons, zested and sliced

5 ml (1 teaspoon) citric acid

Put 1 L (4 cups) water into a pan and bring to a boil. Add the sugar and stir until dissolved. Pour into a large bowl and add the elderflowers, lemons and citric acid. Stir, cover with a tea towel and leave overnight. The next morning, strain through a cheesecloth-lined sieve. Pour into sterilized bottles (see page 53) and store in the fridge or a cool cupboard.

ELDERBERRY & BLACKBERRY CORDIAL

Makes 1.5 L (6 cups)

250 g (9 ounces) elderberries

250 g (9 ounces) blackberries

sugar

juice of 1 lemon

1 cinnamon stick

5 ml (1 teaspoon) citric acid (optional)

Put the berries in a pan with 150 ml (⅔ cup) of water and set over low heat for 5 minutes, or until juice runs from the fruit. Cool, then mash with the back of a spoon. Strain through a jelly bag or a sieve lined with cheesecloth, and measure the juice. Put it back in the pan and add an equal quantity of sugar. Add the lemon juice and cinnamon stick, bring to a boil and boil for 2 minutes. Skim off any scum. Pour into sterilized bottles (see page 53) and seal.

HOW TO MAKE A CORDIAL

Place your fruit in a pan with some water and simmer over low heat until soft. Berries need only a little water, but firm fruits need 200 ml (⅞ cup) to every 500 g (1 pound) of fruit.

Use a cheesecloth-lined sieve or a jelly bag to strain the juicy fruit. Press it through gently with a ladle or the back of a wooden spoon.

Measure the juice and add sugar in the ratio of 350 g (12½ ounces) of sugar (about 425 ml/1¾ cups) to 500 ml (2 cups) of juice. Put back on low heat, stirring to dissolve the sugar, then bring to a boil.

Skim off any scum then pour the cordial into sterilized glass bottles, using a sterilized funnel (see page 53). Store your bottled cordial in the fridge for 1–2 months.

Elderflower syrups, cordials and liqueurs are flavored with the scents of the summer. When pears are abundant in the autumn, this dessert is a reminder of those days. The poached pears are lovely with shortbread.

Serves 4

4 Conference or other firm pears

250 ml (1 cup) elderflower cordial (see page 128)

250 ml (1 cup) water

juice and zest of ½ lemon

4 sprigs fresh mint, to decorate

For the syllabub

250 ml (1 cup) heavy cream (36%)

45 ml (3 tablespoons) elderflower liqueur

POACHED PEARS & ELDERFLOWERS WITH SYLLABUB

Peel the pears, leaving the stems on, and position them snugly in a saucepan. Cover with the cordial, water and lemon juice, cover with a lid and simmer for about 30 minutes, until the pears are soft. Turn them a couple of times during cooking, but be careful not to dent them.

When the pears are ready, transfer them to a plate and keep them in a warm place. Boil the liquid to reduce it to a thin syrup.

To make the syllabub, whip the cream to the soft peak stage and fold in the elderflower liqueur. Put into a small bowl and drizzle a little of the pear syrup over top.

Place each pear on a plate, glaze it with a little syrup, top with a mint sprig and serve with a spoonful of syllabub.

A snug fit

If you grow your own tomatoes, there is a very good chance you will end up with a glut at some stage. This spicy drink is a great way to use them. Some tomatoes are sweeter than others, so always use the ripest you can find.

Serves 4

For the tomato juice (makes about 1.5 L/6 cups)

2 kg (4 pounds) very ripe red tomatoes

6 stalks of celery

½ onion

30 ml (2 tablespoons) sugar (or to taste)

45 ml (3 tablespoons) red wine vinegar

5 ml (1 teaspoon) salt

1 good pinch white pepper

For each drink

1 measure of vodka

1 dash Worcestershire sauce

1 slice lemon

1 stalk celery

BLOODY MARY

To make the tomato juice, core the tomatoes then roughly chop them along with the celery and onion. Put all the ingredients in a large non-reactive pan (stainless steel, not aluminum). Bring to a simmer and cook, uncovered, until the mixture is soft – about 25 minutes – then force the mixture through a sieve. Let the juice cool completely then store in the fridge – it will keep for about 1 week. To keep it longer, return the strained juice to the pan, bring it to a boil and boil for 2–3 minutes. Pour into sterilized bottles (see page 53) and seal tightly.

To make a Bloody Mary, pour the vodka into a tall glass, top up with the tomato juice and add the Worcestershire sauce. Add a slice of lemon and stir with a celery stalk.

A bottle of summer flavor

No air miles for this wine

WINES

What could be better than relaxing in the evening
with a glass of homemade wine? There is not much
in the world that can rival the feeling of absolute
satisfaction, pride and subsequent relaxation. For
a small investment it is easy to make a great deal
of drinkable wine; whether it turns out to be fine
wine, however, very much depends on the care and
patience you put into it. You also have the chance
to try out some exotic recipes that are not available
at any wine merchants we know of, with relatively
little effort. Wine-making can be approached as a scientific experiment
with exact measurements under meticulous conditions or, as we do, much in the
spirit of wine itself, as a vibrant and fun hobby. We are not too bound to strict
rules and prefer to let it evolve naturally. Having said that, there are a few
basics that help achieve a fine wine.

GUIDELINES

- Bottles and all other apparatus must be
  sterilized with boiling water or sterilizing
  solutions. (Campden tablets can be used
  for this.)
- Wines need sugar, yeast, acid and tannin.
  The amounts needed will depend on the
  recipe you use.
- We follow the traditional advice about
  quantities of sugar for wine-making. This
  states that for every 4.5 L (4.75 quarts) of
  grape juice add: 1 kg (2 pounds) of sugar
  (about 1.25 L/5 cups) for a dry wine,
  1.25 kg (2.5 pounds) of sugar (about
  1.560 ml/6¼ cups) for a medium wine,
  and 1.36 kg (2.75 pounds) of sugar (about
  1,625 ml/6½ cups) for a sweet wine.
- Yeast is naturally present in the air all
  around us and also in the "bloom" of
  fruit. You can rely on that to do the job of

fermentation. However, we use good-quality
wine yeast (not baker's yeast) for making
our wines. It is available in granulated or
liquid form and is best bought from a
specialty brewing store or online.
- The crispness of a wine depends on its level
  of acidity. You may need to add more acid
  to wines made from ingredients that aren't
  very acidic, such as flowers or grains. You
  can buy citric acid from brewing stores or
  at old-fashioned drugstores, but we tend to
  use lemon juice, which works fairly well.
- Tannins come from the skin of the grape
  and give the wine that "dry mouth" feel.
  You may need to add extra, depending on
  the type of wine being made. Tannins can be
  bought online or from a brewing store.
- To successfully make wine you need to
  keep the temperature favorable to the vital
  yeasts. During the first fermentation, aim

for 24°C (75°F) and avoid it rising to over 27°C (80°F), when the yeast will start to die, or under 21°C (70°F), when the yeast will be too cold. A warm place, such as your furnace room, is ideal, or you can invest in a heating belt.

MAKING WINE FROM GRAPES

The first step is to press your grapes. The traditional way of doing this is fun but requires removing your socks and cleaning your feet very well. Squish the grapes under your feet and between your toes until they are reduced to pulp and juice. Don't stop until you have squeezed every last bit out of the fruit. Alternatively, use a press: put in a generous layer of grapes wrapped in mesh cloth and then add other layers on top of it until you have used all of your grapes or run out of space.

FERMENTING THE GRAPE JUICE

Once you've pressed the grapes, strain the liquid through a sieve lined with cheesecloth, and then pour it into a fermentation jar or demijohn using a funnel. Put a fermentation lock in the top of the jar, which allows gases to escape but prevents outside air from contaminating the contents.

There are two stages to fermenting your own wines. The first, which lasts for about 10 days, is the frothy, active stage, when the yeasts are multiplying and need air around them. Leave the jar or demijohn three-quarters full for this stage. It is complete when the froth dies back. For the second stage, top the jar up with water and place a fermentation lock on the top. This allows the gases produced during fermentation to escape while keeping air out, thereby avoiding oxidation. It also prevents bacteria and other bugs from ruining your wine.

RACKING THE WINE

Your wine is ready to be racked when the sediment settles and the wine looks clear – it usually takes 8–10 weeks to reach this stage. Racking essentially means siphoning your wine off from above the yeasts (also known as the lees) that have settled at the bottom and transferring it from one container to another. It is important to rack your wine so the lees don't spoil its flavor. To do the siphoning, use a simple length of clear flexible plastic tubing. A month after racking your wine the process should be repeated, and, if you have the patience, do it again 3 weeks later. Before the final racking leave your wine somewhere cold to hasten the settling of any leftover sediment.

BOTTLING & CORKING

When the wine is 6 months old and the fermentation process is complete, you can bottle and cork it. Sterilize your bottles (see page 53), choosing ones made of dark-colored glass to preseve the color of the wine. Use a siphon to pour your wine into the bottles, leaving 4–5 cm (1½–2 inches) at the top for the cork. Cork the bottles using a corking gun or a wooden mallet. Label the bottles clearly and store them on their sides at a temperature of about 13°C (55°F) for a full year.

NOW TRY: PEA POD WINE

To make pea pod wine, place 2 kg (4 pounds) of pea pods in a large pan with 5 L (5 quarts) of water and bring to a boil. Reduce to a simmer for 20 minutes, then remove from the heat, strain off the liquid and add 1 kg (2 pounds) of sugar (about 1.25 L/5 cups), 15 ml (1 tablespoon) of dried yeast, 2 tea bags and a sliced lemon. Cover with a tea towel and leave for 3–4 days, then strain and put into a demijohn with an airlock for 4 weeks. Rack, bottle and cork as above.

HOW TO MAKE WINE FROM GRAPES

First, clean your feet thoroughly, and then put your grapes in a container large enough to stand in.

Press the grapes under your feet until they are reduced to a pulp and you have extracted all the juice.

Put the resulting juice through a sieve lined with cheesecloth to remove any sediment.

Transfer the juice to a sterilized demijohn (see page 53) and allow the natural yeasts to do the fermenting, or use good-quality wine yeast (see page 134).

Line a large colander with open-weave cheesecloths, place into over a large container and pour in the grape juice and pulp.

Twist the cheesecloth tightly and squeeze the juice into the container below. Keep squeezing until you have as much juice as possible.

Add an airlock to your demijohn to keep oxygen out of the fermentation process. The carbon dioxide produced pushes out any oxygen and bubbles away until the sugars in the fruit change to alcohol.

Use plastic tubing to rack your wine, siphoning the wine from above the yeasts that have settled at the bottom into another sterilized demijohn. Store for another month, then rack again. Bottle and cork as described on page 135.

Pea pod wine is a delicious drink, but you can cook with it too. This recipe features a pea-pod wine and mint reduction that is the perfect accompaniment for rolled lamb.

Serves 4

1 knob butter

2 shallots, finely chopped

1 garlic clove, finely chopped

150 g (5 ounces) peas

15 ml (1 tablespoon) chopped fresh mint

15 ml (1 tablespoon) olive oil

salt and freshly ground black pepper

75 g (3 ounces) breadcrumbs (about 125 ml/½ cup)

1 (400 g/13-ounce) breast of lamb

For the reduction

150 ml (⅔ cup) pea pod wine (see page 135)

4-6 fresh mint leaves, finely chopped

15 ml (1 tablespoon) white wine vinegar

15 ml (1 tablespoon) sugar

To serve

roasted potatoes

braised cabbage and pancetta

ROLLED LAMB WITH PEA POD WINE

Preheat the oven to 160°C (325°F). Melt the butter in a pan, add the shallots and garlic, and cook gently until softened. Add the peas, stir for a minute and remove from the heat. Add the mint, olive oil and a pinch of salt and pepper. Put this mixture into a blender with the bread crumbs and blitz for a few seconds.

Lay the breast of lamb out flat and spread the pea stuffing over it. Roll up and tie with butcher's string, and then put the lamb in a roasting pan and roast for 1½ hours.

Meanwhile, make the reduction. Put the wine in a small pan and simmer for 10–15 minutes, until reduced by half. Add the mint leaves, vinegar and sugar and simmer for a further 3–4 minutes. Strain and set aside.

Remove the lamb from the oven, cover with foil and allow to rest for 10 minutes.

Warm the reduction. Slice the lamb, pour the reduction over and serve with roasted potatoes and braised cabbage and pancetta.

No bubbles, all flavor

HARD CIDERS

Hard cider is the fermented juice of apples that have been crushed and then pressed. Every year we make cider with apples from our small orchard, and we also help out our neighbours by taking some of their unwanted apples in exchange for some bottles of cider. On the whole, apples don't last very long unless they are picked when ripe and are not at all bruised or damaged. Making cider means that you can successfully preserve huge quantities of fruit and save lots of money on alcohol by doing so. Cider-making is also a really social activity that can be a great way to pass an autumn day.

CHOOSING APPLES

Any variety of apple can be used to make cider, and even sketchy-looking windfall apples can be turned into good cider. Unless you are growing specific cider-making apples, such as Langworthy, Foxwhelp or Crimson King, which can be brewed on their own, the trick to making a tasty cider is to use a mixture of apples. Use one-third each of bitter-sweet, sweet and sharp apples. A balanced cider should have equal proportions of bitter-sweet apples that are low in acid but high in tannins, such as Dabinett, Somerset Red and Yarlington Mill, sweet dessert apples that have a medium acidity and are low in tannin, such as Cox's Orange Pippin, Golden Delicious and Cornish Gilliflower, and finally some sharper apples with higher acidity, such as Royal Russets or Herefordshire Costards.

PREPARING APPLES

Before you crush your ripe apples, leave them in a heap for 2 or 3 days to soften.

Alternatively, pick up your windfall apples, as they will already be very juicy. Avoid using apples that have serious pest problems, but most apples will generally be usable even if they don't look perfect. These apples will contain some of the natural yeasts, called "bloom," that will ferment later in the process. Apples vary greatly in the amount of juice they create, but on average we would expect to need about 8 kg (17½ pounds) of apples to make 5 L (5 quarts) of cider.

CRUSHING APPLES

Make sure that all your equipment is clean. An electric apple crusher or masticator (see page 142) will enable you to make large volumes of cider quickly and easily, thus adding to the overall enjoyment of the age-old tradition.

Another simple way to crush the apples is to put them in a wooden box and use a spade as a chopper. It needs to be a strong wooden box and the apples should be near the top and closely packed together so they don't easily move. Don't pack it so full that they will jump out and spill on to the floor. Use a sharp, clean spade to chop the apples into small pieces.

PRESSING

Spread your crushed apples out evenly in layers in your press, covering each layer with a sheet of fabric mesh or cheesecloth, and press them so the juice runs straight into a sterilized demijohn or large fermenting bin. This is the time to savor a moment of magic and try the cloudy apple juice before it transforms into a golden alcoholic liquid. If you place a large jug under the press, you can collect some delicious fresh apple juice, which will keep in the fridge for a few days.

When you have squeezed out all the juice from the first batch, unwrap the leftover pulp, also known as the "cheese," and feed it to one of those famous waste-disposal experts, the pigs or the compost bin. Then refill your press and repeat the steps until you have pressed all your apples.

FERMENTING

Once you have your fresh apple juice all stored in demijohns or a large fermenting bin, it's time for the yeast to work its magic. We allow the natural yeasts from the apple skins to do the fermenting, but if you want to ensure success, add a few teaspoons of wine-maker's yeast to the mix. You can also add sugar or syrup to the cider if you prefer a sweeter brew.

BOTTLING

Once fermentation has ceased, any time from 10 days to 1 month, you can transfer the cider straight into bottles for storage using a siphon (see page 137, step 8). At this stage you will often find that a secondary fermentation takes place in the bottle. Cider is usually drunk within a year, but it can be kept for longer. We once bottled some apple juice after trying to pasteurize it, and a couple of months later we were greatly surprised to find it had turned into a bubbly alcoholic drink similar to the fizzy cider produced in Normandy – of course we didn't let on about the mistake to our guests, who loved it!

NOW TRY: PERRY

Wherever the soil is good for growing apple trees, pears will also flourish. To make perry or pear cider, follow exactly the same method as for apple cider, but use pears instead. Perry tends to be much sweeter than cider, so you don't need to add any extra sugar during the fermenting process.

HOW TO MAKE CIDER

Discard any rotten fruit then chop up your apples using a masticator.

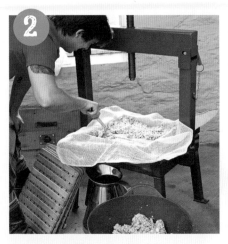

Spoon a layer of the chopped fruit onto a sheet of fabric mesh in your press. The layer should be about 5 cm (2 inches) deep. Fold in the edges of the fabric to make a parcel.

Screw down the press until as much juice as possible has been extracted. If your press is not screwed to the floor, you might need two people to do this: one to hold the press, the other to turn the lever.

Transfer the pressed juice to sterilized demijohns or brewing barrels.

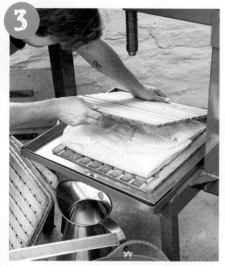

Place a wooden rack on top of the folded fabric. Repeat steps 2 and 3 until you have filled the press, finishing with a wooden rack.

Place a heavy wooden block on top of the final wooden rack, and place a large jug under the spigot.

Add an airlock that allows the gases produced during fermentation to escape but prevents air from getting in to oxidize the cider.

When fermentation is completed and the yeast and sediments have settled at the bottom of the jar, siphon off the good cider into a new demijohn or bottles.

This mussels recipe is our version of *moules marinière* but with a homemade twist. The Armagnac will add a bit of intensity and really bring out the flavor of the cider.

Serves 4

2 kg (4 pounds) mussels, cleaned and beards removed

20 g (¾ ounce) butter (about 22 ml/1½ tablespoons)

140 g (4½ ounces) dry-cured bacon, diced

1 bay leaf

2-3 sprigs of fresh thyme

3 shallots, halved

60 ml (¼ cup) Armagnac (optional)

150 ml (⅔ cup) cider

200 ml (⅞ cup) crème fraîche or sour cream

salt and freshly ground black pepper

MUSSELS WITH CIDER & THYME

Check over the mussels, discarding any that are open or that don't shut when you tap them.

Melt the butter in a large pan, add the bacon and fry for 3–4 minutes. Add the bay leaf, thyme and shallots and cook for a few more minutes. Then add the Armagnac, if using, the mussels and the cider and cook on a high heat for 5 minutes, stirring occasionally.

Remove the mussels from the pan with a slotted spoon when they have all opened. Discard any that are still shut. Simmer the sauce for a few minutes more and stir in the crème fraîche or sour cream. Season well with salt and pepper and serve.

METHOD #23

SAUCES & KETCHUPS

Sauces and ketchups are useful as condiments and can add concentrated flavor to all sorts of dishes. We also find that when it comes to using and preserving vegetables in bulk, they are one of the most effective ways to keep things fresh and tasty. Experiment using the ketchups in your cooking rather than eating them alongside your finished dish: the resulting flavor is much deeper.

PREPARATION

Start by washing or peeling your fruits and vegetables as necessary. Those that are soft enough can then be pureed raw in a blender. Others can be cooked slowly on low heat until soft and then blended. Herbs and chilies often remain more potent if you blitz them right into a sauce. Adding oil, vinegar or citrus juice will help to retain their fresh taste – the amount needed will vary from recipe to recipe.

ADDING FLAVOR

Adding sweetness and spice is best done before you strain the sauce. Use a pestle and mortar to bash up the herbs and spices roughly, and then stir them into the fruit pulp or reduced vegetables to infuse with flavor.

STRAINING

For a thin ketchup, strain through a very fine sieve or a piece of cheesecloth, but for thicker condiments don't worry about some lumps. The key thing is to remove any fragrant whole spices before bottling.

BOTTLING AND STORING

Pour the finished sauce into a sterilized glass bottle (see page 53) and store in the fridge if possible. Consume within 1 month.

GREAT SAUCES

- PESTO SAUCE - This classic combination of basil, olive oil, pine nuts and Parmesan cheese is amazing, but it's also worth experimenting with other ingredients, such as sage and walnuts or parsley and pumpkin seeds. Pesto is excellent for making quick pasta dishes at lunchtime.
- CHILI SAUCE - The hotter the better! You can play around with the ingredients for chili sauce, but a good combination is garlic, ginger, coriander, smoked chilis and vinegar.
- TOMATO KETCHUP - Thicker than other ketchups, this classic is great with loads of dishes. A homemade version really is hard to beat and is a usually made with ripe tomatoes, salt, mace, nutmeg, allspice, cloves, cinnamon, ginger and pepper (see page 127).

HOW TO MAKE MUSHROOM KETCHUP

Makes 400 ml (1⅔ cups)

2 kg (4 pounds) portabello or field mushrooms, chopped

25g (1 ounce) salt (about 30 ml/ 2 tablespoons)

1 small onion, diced

2 whole cloves

5 ml (1 teaspoon) black peppercorns

3-4 allspice berries

310 ml (1¼ cups)white wine vinegar

15 ml (1 tablespoon) soy sauce

15 ml (1 tablespoon) brandy (optional)

If you end up with more than 400 ml (1⅔ cups) of ketchup, reduce it over low heat until the flavor is more intense. It will keep for up to a year.

Put the mushrooms in a shallow dish and cover with salt. Leave for 24 hours, occasionally squashing them and mixing in the salt.

Combine all the other ingredients except the brandy in a pan and bring to a boil. Cover and simmer on medium heat for 1 hour, until you have about 400ml (1⅔ cups) of liquid.

Pass the mixture through a sieve into a jug. Add the brandy, if using. Put a cheesecloth-lined funnel into the neck of a sterilized bottle (see page 53) and pour in the ketchup. Seal tightly and keep in the fridge.

Horseradish and smoked mackerel go brilliantly together, and as canapes these stuffed choux pastry-balls are hard to beat. To make the filling even more quickly, you can use store-bought mayonnaise and horseradish sauce, but we like to make our own. Multiply the recipe, and enjoy the extra sauce with sandwiches.

Makes about 12

2.5 cm (1 inch) horseradish root (more or less, according to how hot you like it and how thick your horseradish is)

100 ml (scant ½ cup) mayonnaise

zest of ½ lemon

2 smoked mackerel fillets, skinned

wedges of lemon, to serve

For the choux pastry

75 g (3 ounces) butter (about 75 ml/⅓ cup)

125 ml (½ cup) water

75 g (3 ounces) flour (about 150 ml/⅔ cup), sifted

2 eggs, beaten

HORSERADISH & SMOKED MACKEREL CHOUX BALLS

Preheat the oven to 220°C (425°F). Line a baking sheet with non-stick baking paper or use a silicone sheet liner.

First, make the choux pastry. Put the butter and water in a medium pan and heat until the butter has melted. Bring to a boil then immediately take off the heat and add the flour all at once. Stir until the mixture pulls away from the sides of the pan to form a ball – don't over-stir at this stage. Allow the mixture to cool down a little, and then add the eggs a little at a time, beating until the mixture forms a smooth dough.

Using two tablespoons or a piping bag fitted with a large tip, put dollops of the dough on the baking sheet, spacing them well apart. Bake for about 20 minutes, until golden brown. Transfer the balls to a wire rack and leave to cool.

Meanwhile, make the filling. Finely grate the horseradish and combine with the mayonnaise and lemon zest. Flake the smoked mackerel then mash it into the horseradish mayonnaise with a fork. Set aside until needed.

When the choux balls are cool, use a small knife to make a slit in the side of each one and pop in a heaped spoonful of the filling. Serve with wedges of lemon.

A little goes a long way

ALCOHOL TINCTURES

It's amazing how many plants have healing qualities, and making tinctures from them is an age-old practice. In the past herb tinctures were household remedies for all sorts of ailments, and they still have their uses today, but never use a tincture if you're pregnant and always consult your doctor first. Alcohol extracts and dissolves the active substance from herbs at the same time as preserving them. Fresh herb tinctures will yield more than dried herb tinctures, so you should really consider growing your own herbs at home.

MAKING FRESH HERB TINCTURES

Tinctures at their most basic involve dissolving a herb or solid in vodka or ethanol. The minimum amount of alcohol required to inhibit the growth of unwanted organisms is 25%, so if you are making your own remedies at home, a typical, standard vodka is more than adequate for the task. Shake the mixture every day for 2 weeks to transfer the herb's qualities to the liquid. When ready, pour the liquid through a piece of cheesecloth and squeeze out every drop.

STORING TINCTURES

Sterilize a small glass bottle (see page 53) and fill it with your tincture. Fit a dropper onto the bottle. Label and store in a dark place. Tinctures can last for years, but the potency will reduce over time.

USING TINCTURES

To use, simply dissolve a few drops in water and drink.

TUMMY TINCTURE

This remedy is ideal for those who suffer from indigestion. Take it after eating, or beforehand to stimulate your digestive enzymes and promote absorption of good nutrients.

100 g (3½ ounces) fresh rosemary

90 g (3¼ ounces) fresh bay leaves

400 ml (1⅔ cups) vodka

To make the tincture, follow the numbered steps opposite.

HOW TO MAKE A HERBAL TINCTURE

Pick your herbs, wash well and allow them to dry. Chop the herbs finely.

Place the chopped herbs in a large jar and pour the vodka over them.

Close the lid tightly and shake the jar well. Continue to shake the jar daily for at least 2 weeks.

Strain the contents through a cheesecloth-lined sieve into a jug, and squeeze out as much of the liquid as possible. Store the tincture in sterilized dark-colored dropper bottles (see page 53).

Propolis is a sticky resin that bees collect, and it has fantastic antiseptic properties. We have been making this drink to help with sore throats and infections since we first started keeping bees many years ago. You can use it in varying amounts, depending on how sore your throat is feeling. We find it incredibly effective.

For the tincture

10 g (½ ounce) propolis

30 ml (2 tablespoons) vodka

For the drink

4-6 drops propolis tincture

5-10 ml (1-2 teaspoons) honey

1 slice lemon

4 whole cloves

a sprig of fresh thyme

1-2 fresh sage leaves

BEE HEALTHY PROPOLIS DRINK

To make the tincture, place the propolis in a jar, add the vodka and shake every day for 2–3 weeks, until all the propolis has dissolved. Strain the liquid through a coffee filter to remove any bits of bee barb that may have got mixed with the propolis. Transfer to a sterilized glass bottle (see page 53) and store in a dark place.

To make the propolis drink, simply put 6–8 drops of the tincture in a mug, add the honey, lemon, cloves, thyme and sage and top up with boiling water.

soothes a sore throat

5

FREEZING

FREEZING

Enzyme activity within food cells, or bacterial activity from outside, means that no food will keep indefinitely in its natural form: everything is subject to the processes of decay and deterioration. The idea behind all forms of preservation is either to inhibit the activity of disease-causing microorganisms, or to kill them altogether. Keeping food in the refrigerator will slow down bacterial action, but freezing it can stop stop the action entirely, since frozen bacteria are completely inactive. This means you can enjoy your frozen produce for longer.

GUIDELINES

- Use the correct type of packaging or container and ensure that the food is tightly wrapped or sealed.
- As with all preserving, ensure the food is in perfect condition.
- Divide the food into small portions to ensure rapid freezing and that smaller ice crystals are formed – the defrosted food will be of better quality.
- Label items clearly, including their expiration date (see chart on page 159).
- Check that your freezer is operating at −18°C (0°F).
- Don't try to freeze too many unfrozen items at once.
- Leave space around any new items that have been put into the freezer so that cold air can circulate. Pack them more tightly once they are completely frozen.
- Restock your freezer regularly – a full freezer is more efficient than a half-empty one.
- Defrost items in the fridge.
- Visit the freezer before you go shopping – use your own top-quality produce rather than spending money at the supermarket.

FREEZING BASICS

While refrigerators have a minimal effect on the texture of food, you do have to be a little more aware of the consequences of freezing. The cells in food contain a great deal of water, and the majority of foods will freeze solid at −5°C (23°F). If it is done correctly, freezing has little adverse impact on the quality of raw cuts of meat and minimal effect on most vegetables. However, freezing can completely change the texture of some types of fruit, which can become soft and mushy when defrosted.

If the food is frozen slowly, the water will form large ice crystals, which can break through the walls of the cells and will affect the texture of the produce. When the food is subsequently thawed, much of the liquid can drain out of these damaged cells, taking with it some of the minerals and vitamins and destroying the food's unique taste and texture. Rapid freezing causes smaller ice crystals to form, so the damage to the cells is minimized and, once thawed, the resultant food is much closer to its original state.

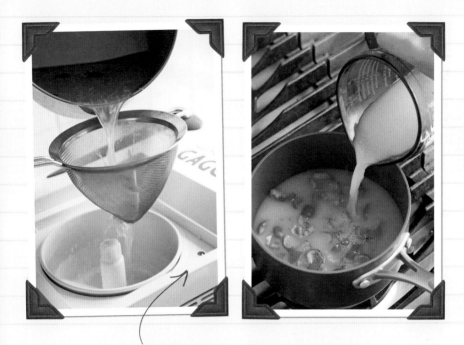

Invest in an ice-cream maker – you'll enjoy it

Orange zest adds a lovely citrusy flavor

ORGANIZATION

It is quite common to fill your freezer with fresh produce, forget all about it and only discover it again months – if not years – later. Freezers need to be well organized, as it's not worth going to the trouble of processing your food if you are going to store it, lose it in the depths of your freezer and end up throwing it away. That is why we prefer an upright freezer to a chest freezer. The shelves and compartments make it that much simpler to stock effectively, to keep a clear overview of your supplies and to quickly locate and remove the food you want to use.

PACKAGING

It is essential that the food going into the freezer be tightly and carefully wrapped in moisture-proof or vapor-proof containers or materials. Expel as much air as possible from any packaging. Make sure that no air can enter and that no moisture can escape or evaporate from the package. With a little care, anything frozen at its optimum freshness should emerge from the freezer in perfect condition.

If you pack and wrap your foods properly, you can avoid freezer burn, which leads to a loss of nutrients, flavor, color, texture, taste, moisture and quality. Food that has been attacked by freezer burn loses moisture, is covered in frost and will have grayish-white spots or patches on the surface. Similar deterioration may occur if the food comes into contact with air. In most cases the burnt food is still edible – it is possible to cut away affected areas before or after the food has been defrosted, but the food will be dry and tough. Food can also be affected by freezer burn if it is stored for too long.

Clearly label your items: include the date on which they were frozen as well as the date by which they should be used (see chart below).

DEFROSTING

Having arrested bacteria growth in the freezer for the duration of the storage, we should not forget that it can take hold again once the product is being thawed. As soon as food begins to defrost, the temperature rises, and, as moisture is present, bacteria will start to grow. If the food is thawed at a temperature above 5°C (40°F), bacteria will multiply rapidly in a very short time and can lead to food poisoning. For this reason, it is very important to defrost food safely, preferably overnight in the refrigerator.

STORAGE TIMES

If your freezer is set to an energy-efficient −18°C (0°F), most goods can be kept for up to 3 months. With a lower temperture setting of −30°C (−22°F), you can store some items for up to 1 year – use this chart as your maximum guideline.

FOODSTUFF	STORING TIME
RAW VEGETABLES	12 months
RAW MEAT	12 months
RAW WHITE FISH	6–12 months
RAW OILY FISH	4 months
UNCOOKED PASTRY	3–6 months
COOKED FOOD	2 months

METHOD #25

ICE CREAMS

There is almost no limit to the flavorings you can add to ice cream to personalize it. Indeed, the bases for ice creams are varied as well, from lighter ones made with milk to those made with heavy cream. For us, however, the flavor and texture of a custard-based ice cream is very hard to beat -- and a simple vanilla ice cream is one of our favorites. The easiest way to make ice cream is to use an ice-cream maker, but we've provided instructions for making ice cream by hand as well.

HAND-MAKING ICE CREAM

Make a custard (see steps 1–4) then add your chosen flavoring. Put your liquid ice cream into a lidded plastic container and place in the freezer for about 2 hours, until the liquid freezes at the edges. Empty the contents into a bowl and whisk to break down the ice crystals. Return the ice cream to the container and place in the freezer for another couple of hours. Repeat these steps up to three times to get creamy ice cream.

VANILLA ICE CREAM

Makes about 625 ml (2½ cups)

250 ml (1 cup) milk

1 vanilla bean, split in half

4 egg yolks

100 g (3½ ounces) superfine sugar (about 125 ml/½ cup)

250 ml (1 cup) heavy cream (36%)

To make the ice cream, follow the numbered steps on this page and opposite.

HOW TO MAKE ICE CREAM

Put the milk and vanilla bean in a pan over low heat. Bring to a simmer but do not allow it to boil. Turn off the heat and allow the milk to stand for 20 minutes, then remove the vanilla bean and scrape the seeds into the milk.

Put the egg yolks and sugar in a bowl and beat until creamy. Add 30 ml (2 tablespoons) of the flavored milk to the eggs and beat in. Add 30 ml (2 tablespoons) of milk and stir well.

Slowly add the rest of the milk, stirring continuously. Return the mixture to the pan and heat very gently, stirring until thick. Do not allow it to boil.

Remove from the heat and set aside. At this point you can add fruit or a liqueur of your choice, but remember that if you use too much alcohol, the ice cream will not set firm.

When cool, stir in the cream and either follow the instructions for your ice-cream maker or finish the ice cream by hand (see page 160). Store in the freezer for up to 3 months.

This is our version of raspberry ripple. Adding herbs or spices to your ice creams can create some really unusual flavors. Here the addition of sage turns an old classic into something a little more sophisticated.

Serves 8-10

2 large eggs

150 g (5 ounces) superfine sugar (about 175 ml/³⁄₄ cup)

500 ml (2 cups) heavy cream (36%)

2 fresh sage leaves, stems removed, finely shredded

300 g (10 ounces) raspberries

15 ml (1 tablespoon) confectioners' sugar

For the shortbread

200 g (7 ounces) flour (about 400 ml/1²⁄₃ cups)

100 g (3½ ounces) unsalted butter (about 105 ml/7 tablespoons)

75 g (3 ounces) confectioners' sugar (about 150 ml/²⁄₃ cup)

2 fresh sage leaves, main stalk removed, finely chopped

RASPBERRY & SAGE ICE CREAM WITH SHORTBREAD

Whisk the eggs in a large bowl until light and frothy, then gradually add the superfine sugar and whisk for 2 more minutes. Pour in the cream and whisk well. Once mixed, stir in the shredded sage leaves.

Pour the mixture into an ice-cream maker and freeze to a soft-scoop consistency according to the manufacturer's instructions. Alternatively, follow the instructions on page 160.

Meanwhile, place the raspberries and confectioners' sugar in a bowl and crush them lightly with the back of a fork. When the ice cream has frozen to a soft-scoop consistency, gently fold in the raspberries to create a rippled effect. Transfer to a plastic container and freeze until solid.

To make the shortbread, preheat the oven to 160°C (325°F). Put the flour, butter and confectioners' sugar in a food processor and whizz until the mixture looks like bread crumbs. Take out the blade and mix in the chopped sage leaves.

Press the mixture into a small baking pan, about 20×15cm (8×6 inches). Bake for 20 minutes, until golden. Cut up the shortbread in the pan, then place on a rack to cool.

Serve the ice cream with a slice of shortbread.

Instantly refreshing

SORBET

A sorbet is a semi-frozen mixture of fruit juice or puree and sugar syrup, and it is softer and grainier than ice cream. We love to make them regularly as a great way to preserve that succulent quality and intense freshness that you get from a fruit when it's in season. It may sound a bit fancy, but cleansing your palate with a homemade seasonal sorbet is a great way to break up a meal. Alternatively serve up a decent scoop as a dessert and enjoy with fresh berries or a warm slice of cake.

CHOOSING INGREDIENTS

The key to a good sorbet is to use tasty ingredients. You can make a sorbet out of just about anything, but fruit in particular lends itself to this preserving method. You want the liquid to become an amalgamation of flavors.

STRAINING

Sorbets are often clean-tasting with a zing from the ice-cold crystals and intense fruit flavor. Straining your sorbet mixture through a fine sieve before it goes in the machine keeps it clear. If you want to add any extra texture, do this at the end.

ALCOHOL

Although alcohol doesn't freeze, it is often used when making a sorbet. Apart from adding flavor, it also makes the finished sorbet less grainy and smoother to eat. If you don't want a flavored alcohol to mess with your sorbet but you still want it to have a "kick", vodka is the most discreet alcohol to use.

ORANGE & ROSE HIP SORBET

Makes 750 ml (3 cups)

750 g (1½ pound) rose hips

250 ml (1 cup) water

250 g (8 ounces) sugar (about 325 ml/1⅓ cups) plus extra, to taste

500 ml (2 cups) orange juice

zest of 2 oranges

30 ml (2 tablespoons) vodka

To make the sorbet, follow the numbered steps opposite.

HOW TO MAKE ORANGE & ROSEHIP SORBET

Skin or peel the rose hips. Put them in a pan with water, sugar, and orange juice and zest, and simmer until soft and the juices have been released. Strain through a fine sieve.

Sweeten the solution with your extra sugar, if necessary, and add spices or any further flavors. Finally, allow to cool.

Add the vodka to the fruity sugar solution, or lace the ice-cream maker with a generous shot before adding the mixture.

If using a machine, follow the manufacturer's instructions. If making by hand, see page 160. Store in the freezer for up to 3 months.

Savoury fruits, such as tomatoes, can really shine when you eat them in a different way, and this sorbet is delicious with the fresh salsa and toasted brioche beneath. It makes for an impressive starter or a special lunch.

Serves 4

3 ripe avocados

400 g (13 ounces) cooked white crab meat

1 fresh red chili, finely chopped

15 ml (1 tablespoon) chopped fresh cilantro

3 spring onions, finely chopped

5 ml (1 teaspoon) sesame seeds

salt and freshly ground black pepper

For the sorbet

100 g (3½ ounces) sugar (about 125ml/½ cup)

100 ml (scant ½ cup) water

30 ml (2 tablespoons) olive oil

1 onion, finely chopped

5 ml (1 teaspoon) orange zest

1 sprig fresh thyme

1 kg (2 pound) tomatoes, seeded and finely chopped

6-8 fresh basil leaves

5 ml (1 teaspoon) salt

For the dressing

5 ml (1 teaspoon) sesame oil

5 ml (1 teaspoon) crushed fresh ginger

5 ml (1 teaspoon) honey

juice of 1 lime

4 slices of toasted brioche, to serve

CRAB SALSA WITH TOMATO SORBET

First make the sorbet. Put the sugar and water in a small pan, bring to a boil, then simmer until the volume has reduced by half. Set aside to cool.

Heat the olive oil in a pan and add the onion, orange zest and thyme. Cook until the onions are soft but not colored. Add half the tomatoes and all the basil, and cook for 5–10 minutes or until the water has evaporated and the mixture has thickened. Remove from the heat, discard the thyme sprig and blend in a food processor or blender with the rest of the tomatoes, the salt and the reserved sugar syrup until smooth. Pass through a fine sieve into a bowl. Transfer it to an ice-cream maker for 10 minutes of stirring and chiling, and then put it in the freezer for 2–3 hours. If making by hand, follow the instructions on page 160.

To make the salsa, spoon the avocado flesh into a mixing bowl. Add the crab, chili, cilantro, spring onions and sesame seeds, season with salt and pepper and mix gently together. Whisk the dressing ingredients together in a bowl.

Place a slice of toasted brioche on each plate, add some spoonfuls of salsa, drizzle with the dressing and top with a scoop of tomato sorbet.

The taste relationship between orange and chocolate is dangerously addictive. To give the classic combination a fiery edge, we use chili chocolate in the brownies, but any good chocolate will do.

Serves 4

150 g (5 ounces) flour (about 310 ml/1¼ cups)

5 ml (1 teaspoon) baking powder

200 g (7 ounces) dark chocolate, broken into squares

250 g (8 ounces) butter (about 250 ml/1 cup), diced

300 g (10 ounces) superfine sugar (about 375 ml/ 1½ cups)

4 large eggs, beaten

100 g (3½ ounces) walnuts

150 g (5 ounces) chili chocolate, broken into small pieces

For the sorbet

200 g (7 ounces) sugar (about 250 ml/1 cup)

200 ml (⅞ cup) water

juice from 6 large oranges (about 400ml/1⅔ cups)

1 whole star anise

zest of 1 orange, cut into small strips

CHILI CHOCOLATE BROWNIES WITH ORANGE SORBET

First make the sorbet. Put the sugar and water into a medium pan, bring to a boil, then reduce the heat and simmer for 10–15 minutes or until the volume has reduced by half. Add the orange juice and star anise, bring back to a boil, then turn off the heat and allow to cool. When cool, strain through a fine sieve and place in your ice-cream maker along with the orange zest. Freeze according to the manufacturer's instructions. Alternatively, make by hand as described on page 160.

Preheat the oven to 180°C (350°F). Line a 45×25×5 cm (18×10×2 inch) cake pan with parchment paper, or grease it with butter.

Sift the flour and baking powder together into a bowl. Put the dark chocolate and butter into a heatproof bowl over a pan of simmering water. Allow to melt, then remove from the heat and stir in the sugar. Mix in the eggs and finally fold in the flour mixture, walnuts and chili chocolate.

Spread the mixture into the cake pan and bake for 20 minutes. Leave to cool in the pan, then remove and cut into squares.

Serve each brownie topped with a scoop of orange sorbet.

INDEX

ACKNOWLEDGMENTS

PICTURE CREDITS

All photographs © **Nick Pope** with the exception of the following: **Fotolia**/Monica Butnaru (used throughout). **Strawbridge Family Archive** 20 (left). **Thinkstock**/iStockphoto (used throughout).

Illustrations: **Abigail Read** 41, 53, 56, 63, 94, 97, 110. **Charlotte Strawbridge** 16, 28, 48, 122, 154. **James Strawbridge** 39.

Publisher: Stephanie Jackson
Managing Editor: Clare Churly
Copy-editor: Annie Lee
Creative Director: Jonathan Christie
Designer: Jaz Bahra
Illustrators: Abigail Read, Charlotte Strawbridge, James Strawbridge
Photographer: Nick Pope
Stylist: Alison Clarkson
Kitchen Dogsbody: Jim Tomson
Production Manager: Pete Hunt